AMERICA the BEAUTIFUL
GEORGIA

by Zachary A. Kent

Consultants

Gwen Hutcheson, Coordinator, Social Studies, Georgia Department of Education

Edward J. Cashin, Ph.D., Professor of History, Augusta College

John D. Duncan, Ph.D., Professor of History, Armstrong State College

Robert L. Hillerich, Ph.D., Bowling Green State University, Bowling Green, Ohio

℗ CHILDRENS PRESS®

CHICAGO

Atlanta at night

Project Editor: Joan Downing
Assistant Editor: Shari Joffe
Design Director: Margrit Fiddle
Typesetting: Graphic Connections, Inc.
Engraving: Liberty Photoengraving

Childrens Press®, Chicago
Copyright © 1988 by Regensteiner Publishing Enterprises, Inc.
All rights reserved. Published simultaneously in Canada.
Printed in the United States of America.
1 2 3 4 5 6 7 8 9 10 R 97 96 95 94 93 92 91 90 89 88

Library of Congress Cataloging-in-Publication Data

Kent, Zachary.
  America the beautiful, Georgia.

  (America the beautiful state books)
  Includes index.
  Summary: Introduces the geography, history,
government, economy, industry, culture, historic sites,
and famous people of the largest state in area east of
·the Mississippi.
  1. Georgia—Juvenile literature. [1. Georgia]
I. Title. II. Series.
F286.3.K46 1988   975.8   87-35455
ISBN 0-516-00456-5

An oak-lined road on Cumberland Island

TABLE OF CONTENTS

Chapter 1

IN PRAISE OF GEORGIA

IN PRAISE OF GEORGIA

Georgia, Georgia, the whole day
through,
Just an old sweet song keeps Georgia
on my mind.

Georgians chose "Georgia On My Mind" as their state song in 1979. The dreamy lyrics of the popular melody suggest a place of irresistible charm. Georgia is certainly that, but it is also much more. In fact, part of the state's allure is its very diversity.

The "Peach State," the "Goober State," "Empire State of the South"—if Georgians have yet to pick one special nickname, it is because so many favorite ones apply. Located deep in the heart of the South, the rich and unusual qualities of Georgia's land and resources make it stand out among the states.

Chief among Georgia's assets are a people varied in background, interests, and goals. With blood and glory, pride and shame, energy and ideas, Georgians have stitched together a unique and colorful patchwork heritage. It is the spirit of Georgia's farmers, factory workers, pioneers, poets, and politicians that ultimately makes Georgia a land of progress and productivity.

Chapter 2
THE LAND

THE LAND

"It abounds with Rivers, Woods, and Meadows. . . . The air is healthy and the soil in general fruitful, and of infinite variety." This is how Scottish Baronet Sir Robert Montgomery described the Georgia region in 1717. Today, among those states located east of the Mississippi River, Georgia is the largest, covering an area of 58,910 square miles (152,583 square kilometers). Of the fifty states, it stands twenty-first in size. Georgia stretches 315 miles (507 kilometers) from north to south and 250 miles (402 kilometers) from east to west.

The land that makes up Georgia boasts many striking features. Streams that course through the northern mountains form into valley lakes. Rivers flow ceaselessly toward the sea past rolling plateaus dotted with farms and orchards. The dry flatlands and woods of the central part of the state gradually give way to marshes and swamps along the Atlantic Ocean. At last, along 100 miles (161 kilometers) of coastline, fresh water mingles with salt water, and ocean waves crash upon the sandy beaches of a dozen islands.

TOPOGRAPHY

Millions of years ago, all of Georgia lay beneath a vast ocean. In time, the continuous upheaval of the earth's crust thrust

The lush Blue Ridge Mountains occupy Georgia's northeast corner.

mountain ranges above the water's surface. Gradually, the ocean receded, exposing more of the floor beneath it. Today, Georgia's topography (the shape of the land) can be divided into three sections: the northern mountains, the Piedmont Plateau, and the coastal plain.

The Blue Ridge Mountains, part of the great Appalachian range of mountains and valleys, occupy the northeast part of the state. The jutting peak of Brasstown Bald Mountain, at 4,784 feet (1,458 meters), marks Georgia's highest point.

South of the mountain region, covering 30 percent of the state, lies the Piedmont Plateau. The gentle hills of the Piedmont provide farmers with some of Georgia's most fertile land. A series of low ridges called the Fall Line Hills, which can be traced from Augusta through Macon to Columbus, separate the Piedmont Plateau from the state's largest region, the coastal plain.

Vegetation on Cumberland Island, one of Georgia's coastal islands

In prehistoric times, the tides of a great ocean once beat against the shore of Georgia's Fall Line. The slow withdrawal of this ocean left behind an extensive coastal plain that covers the entire southern half of the state. Over a distance of 150 miles (241 kilometers), Georgia's broad, flat plains drop only 500 feet (152 meters) to sea level at the coast. On one terrace of land, ancient ocean waters became trapped. Indians called this boggy place the Okefenokee, "Land of the Trembling Earth." Today, the Okefenokee Swamp, located in the southeastern corner of the state and extending into Florida, is the second-largest freshwater swamp in the United States. Farther to the east, where the coastal plain meets the Atlantic Ocean, river silts and ocean tides have acted to form a string of islands. Called the Golden Isles, they are part of the Sea Islands chain.

Georgia's abundant pine forests (left) are tapped for gum resin (right), which is refined into such products as turpentine, pine oil, resin, and tar.

The loamy sands and clays that cover the surface of the state vary in color from chocolaty brown to red, orange, and yellow. Even today, farmers plowing Georgia's red clay sometimes find fish fossils to remind them that their land once lay beneath a sea.

THE PINES

Forests cover more than two-thirds of Georgia's land area. The most common trees in these woods are pines. The Piedmont hills and the northern mountains are the most densely wooded areas. The shortleaf, loblolly, longleaf, and slash varieties of pine are important in the production of lumber and pulp. Longleaf and slash pines also provide gums that can be refined into turpentine, rosin, tar, and pitch. Because of their once-essential value in shipbuilding, these pine products are still called "naval stores." Georgia conservationists sometimes plant hardy Virginia pines to stop erosion in open, sandy regions. Squat and scrubby, these trees put down roots that hold the soil together.

Dozens of other kinds of trees flourish in the state as well. In the southern swamps, tall cypress trees stand among willows, cottonwoods, and cedars. Georgians have chosen the impressive live oak, which flourishes on the southern coastal plain, as their state tree. Along the northern hills and mountains, other hardwoods, such as red and white oaks, hickories, birches, beeches, and maples, take their place among the pines. The blossoms of magnolia, dogwood, and elderberry trees help make Georgia a colorful and fragrant region in springtime. Roses, hibiscus, azaleas, and poinsettias bloom throughout the coastal area. Cattails and saltgrass grow thickly in the marshlands. Across the open plains, one can find wiregrass and many kinds of wildflowers.

WILDLIFE

When European settlers first pushed west into central Georgia, they discovered great tracts of grassy, open plain. Grazing on these prairies, as far as the eye could see, were herds of buffalo. Although the complete slaughter of Georgia's buffalo occurred before 1800, many other wild animals have survived to take refuge in Georgia's parks and preserves. More than forty species of mammals make Georgia their home. They range from fox and opossum in the mountains, to wild boar and muskrat in the swamps. White-tailed deer can be found throughout the state, and black bears can be spotted in the northern mountains and the Okefenokee Swamp. Georgia's reptiles and amphibians include many kinds of frogs, toads, salamanders, and non-poisonous snakes. Alligators lie half-submerged in sluggish river and swamp waters, while poisonous snakes such as the coral, copperhead, and water moccasin sun themselves on the banks nearby.

Among the many plants and animals that can be found in Georgia are wild turkeys, azaleas, opossums, mountain laurels, alligators, rat snakes, gayfeathers, and white-tailed deer.

A rushing stream at Amicalola Falls State Park

From bald eagle to osprey, the variety of birds in Georgia is mind-boggling. Tiny St. Simons Island, for example, boasts a bird list of well over two hundred species.

RIVERS AND LAKES

Seventeen major rivers flow through Georgia. Those in the eastern half of the state flow into the Atlantic Ocean, while those in the west course down to the Gulf of Mexico. The Savannah, St. Marys, and Chattahoochee rivers help form the eastern, southern, and western borders of the state respectively. Other rivers include the Ogeechee, Canoochee, Altamaha, Ohoopee, Oconee, Satilla, Ocmulgee, Alapaha, Withlacoochee, Ochlockonee, and Flint.

In the northern Blue Ridge region, the Etowah and Oostanaula rivers rush through mountain twists and turns with startling beauty. The lazy Suwannee River, which snakes through the

Okefenokee Swamp, is the same "Swanee River" celebrated in Stephen Foster's famous song.

In the 1930s, engineers embarked on a massive program to build dams across many of Georgia's rivers. When finished, these dams provided Georgians with flood control, improved irrigation, and hydroelectric power stations. They also resulted in the formation of the largest lakes in the state. Clark Hill Lake on the Savannah River is the biggest, covering 70,000 acres (28,328 hectares). Among Georgia's other artificial lakes are Hartwell, Sinclair, Sidney Lanier, Allatoona, Seminole, and Harding.

CLIMATE

Normally, Georgians enjoy lovely, temperate weather. Average temperatures range from a mild 45 degrees Fahrenheit (7.2 degrees Celsius) in January to a balmy 82 degrees Fahrenheit (27.7 degrees Celsius) in July. The state's warm climate, healthy rainfall levels, and rich soil add up to fine growing conditions and long planting seasons for farmers. Southern Georgia experiences as many as three hundred frost-free days of weather each year. Most Georgians seldom see snow during their brief winters; 1.5 inches (3.8 centimeters) is the state's annual average. When the weather does turn cold, it often catches Georgians by surprise. The slightest icing causes massive traffic jams and sends cars without snow tires skidding off the roads.

Hurricanes born in the Gulf of Mexico have been known to tear across Georgia from time to time. In the spring of 1986, a tornado touched down in Cobb County, damaging a hundred homes. When heat waves occur in Georgia, lack of rainfall causes severe drought conditions. Crops wither beneath the scorching sun, sometimes leaving farmers with nothing left to harvest.

Chapter 3

THE PEOPLE

THE PEOPLE

"The farm is mine again," Oscar Lorick of Cochran, Georgia proclaimed joyously. Lorick's farm had been owned by his family for 119 years. In the fall of 1985, however, he had been in danger of losing it. When he was unable to repay a mortgage loan, the lending bank threatened to evict him. During the next six months, Lorick traveled the state telling his sad story. Generous Georgians responded by donating the entire $75,000 he needed. On April 12, 1986, Lorick was able to pay off his mortgage, burn the bank-loan note, and fully reclaim his farm.

Georgians are often proud and independent people. More than anything, they understand a person's deep attachment to his land. It is Georgia's country farmers who have provided the state with one of its several nicknames, the "Cracker State."

Georgia country folk have been called "Crackers" for as long as two hundred years. Although some Georgians are proud of the nickname, others object to it because it is sometimes used as a disparaging term for poor, southern whites. Some say that the term arose because Georgia farm families once commonly crushed or "cracked" corn to make hominy grits or cornmeal.

Another story describes how Georgia farmers piled wagons high with their crops at harvest time. As they drove these mule-team wagons to markets outside the state, they amused themselves by popping and cracking their whips. Some were quite skilled, and when asked to identify themselves, they proudly announced that they were whipcrackers from Georgia.

Whatever the true origin of the nickname, as long as Georgians till the soil, there surely will be Georgia Crackers.

POPULATION

Georgia had 5,463,105 people when the 1980 census was taken—a figure that rose to 5,976,000 according to estimates in 1985. This makes Georgia the eleventh-most-populous state. Between 1970 and 1980, the United States' overall population grew by 11.45 percent. During the same period, Georgia's population rose by 19.1 percent. It is a simple fact that Georgia's warm climate and booming business opportunities are drawing Americans from other states. Forecasts predict that by the year 2000, more than 6.5 million people will be living in Georgia.

Since the days of its colonization, Georgia's white population has been predominantly of Anglo-Saxon descent. The days of slavery, however, witnessed the forced arrival of many thousands of African slaves. As late as 1890, blacks represented 45 percent of Georgia's population. News of well-paying jobs in northern factories sparked a heavy migration of blacks from the state between 1910 and 1950. In recent years, this trend has leveled off. Though reduced to 27 percent of the state's total population in 1980, 1,465,000 blacks still reside in Georgia.

The size of Georgia's foreign-born population remains small. The 1980 census showed that among Georgia's 91,480 foreigners are Mexicans, Puerto Ricans, Cubans, Koreans, Chinese, Japanese, Filipinos, Vietnamese, and people of many European countries. As its cities become more cosmopolitan, Georgia's foreign-born population can be expected to continue to grow.

Religion plays an important role in the lives of many Georgians. Small but growing numbers of Roman Catholics and Jews live in the state. Of the Protestant denominations, Baptists have by far the largest membership. Nearly two of every three Georgians attend a Baptist church. In the 1730s, John Wesley preached in Frederica and Savannah before returning to England to found the Methodist church. Today, Methodists represent the state's second-largest religious group. Other Protestant denominations represented in Georgia are Presbyterian, Episcopalian, Congregational, and Disciples of Christ.

POPULATION DISTRIBUTION

Twentieth-century agricultural methods have enabled a shrinking number of Georgia farmers to produce ever-higher crop yields. At the same time, factory whistles increasingly beckon rural Georgians to employment in the cities. In 1920, for example, three-quarters of Georgia's population still lived on farms or in small towns. Through the years, that figure has shifted so dramatically that today, two-thirds of the population live in urban areas.

The 1980 census reported that Atlanta, with a population of 425,022, remains by far the largest city in the state. Fulton, DeKalb, and other surrounding counties have developed so quickly that in 1986, greater Atlanta accounted for 37 percent of Georgia's residents.

Georgia's oldest city is Savannah, situated near the mouth of the Savannah River. Albany, in the southwestern part of the state, is another important city. Most of Georgia's urban growth, however, has occurred on the Piedmont Plateau. Macon, located in the very center of the state, attracts workers to its cotton-textile mills. The city of Athens grew up around the campus of the University of Georgia. Augusta, also on the Piedmont Plateau, shares its metropolitan population with South Carolina just across the Savannah River. Conversely, many people who work in Columbus, Georgia's second-largest city, commute from Alabama suburbs.

REGIONALISM

North of Atlanta, Georgians call a burlap bag a "tow sack." South of that city, the same bag is often identified as a "croker sack." Farmers in the Blue Ridge region split "lightwood" in order to start winter fires. A visitor to coastal Georgia, however, might be surprised to hear the same kindling wood called "fatwood." Such differences in dialect help give Georgians a very real feeling of regionalism.

Regional varieties in speech within the state date back more than 150 years. Whereas Georgia's earliest pioneers were European, many of the state's later arrivals came from the northeastern states. New Englanders and others who settled in the Blue Ridge Mountains and the Piedmont Plateau during the 1820s and 1830s brought along their own habits, vocabularies, and accents. Though they soon considered themselves genuine Georgians, they still retained rich flavorings of their own special heritages.

Immediately after the Civil War, Yankee businessmen flocked to Atlanta to take advantage of its growing economy. Today, job opportunities in Georgia's cities continue to entice Yankees southward. Some native Georgians liken this trend to a second invasion of their state.

The regional differences in customs and outlook that

The people of Georgia are involved in a variety of economic activities, including peanut farming (left) and egg production (above).

distinguish northern Georgians from their southern Georgia neighbors are easily noticed by travelers. Above the Fall Line Hills, the state's cities bustle with manufacturing activity. On the southern coastal plains, however, the warm climate tends to slow things down, and life seems to proceed at a much more relaxed and casual pace.

Regionalism even extends into the lives of Georgia's farmers. Drive twenty miles (thirty-two kilometers) in any direction from Gainesville and you will hear farmers discussing chicken and egg production. Across central Georgia, growing conditions for soybeans, peaches, and cotton are the farmers' greatest concern. Down in Mitchell and adjacent southwest Georgia counties, however, talk revolves around peanuts and pecans.

There is nothing wrong with the regionalism that endures in Georgia. In fact, the differences that exist within the state are what make it such an interesting place.

Chapter 4
THE BEGINNING

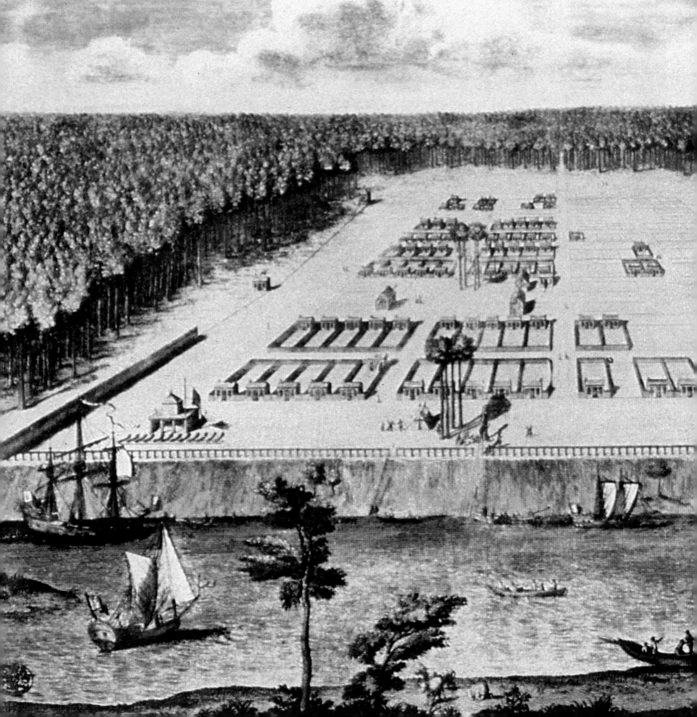

THE BEGINNING

THE ORIGINAL GEORGIANS

Although stone tools dating back as far as 10,000 B.C. have been discovered in the southeastern United States, little is known about the hunters and gatherers who first ventured into what is now Georgia. The mystery of this region's natives is intensified by surviving reminders of their cultures. In Putnam County near Eatonton, a giant eagle made from stones stretches more than 100 feet (30.5 meters) across the ground. Near Chatsworth, a thick, crude defense wall extends for 1,500 feet (457 meters) around the crest of Fort Mountain. Most unusual of all are the many earth mounds scattered throughout the state.

Archaeologists think Georgia's Mound Builders may have appeared as early as 8000 B.C. Beside rivers and streams, they constructed pyramids that are flattened at the top and rise as high as sixty feet (eighteen meters). Though usually made of dirt, some of the mounds consist of piled shells, sometimes in the form of rings or circles. In the shadows of these man-made hills, organized tribal towns flourished for centuries. Diggers have discovered pottery shards, arrowheads, and skeletal remains at these sites. Yet no one knows for sure whether the mounds were used as places of worship, burial grounds, or lookouts. Today, visitors can examine surviving mounds at a number of sites,

This effigy figure (left) was one of the artifacts uncovered at Etowah Mounds (right), site of an Indian culture that thrived from about A.D. 1000 to 1500.

including Etowah Mounds near Cartersville and Kolomoki Mounds in southwestern Georgia.

Gradually, the civilization of the Mound Builders passed out of existence. Archaeologists theorize that as early as A.D. 1000, other wandering, warlike groups began to invade the region. The Cherokee, sometimes called the "cave people" because of their hillside dwellings, entered the mountain country from the north. From the southwest, people of the Muskhogean culture pushed forward, conquering and absorbing the Mound Builders they encountered. When the English later noticed that these natives often lived beside streams, they gave them the name "Creek" Indians.

DE SOTO'S TREASURE HUNT

The Cherokee and Creek thrived on their new lands. From the mountain woods to the coastal marshes, they found a territory plentiful with wild game. Using bows and arrows, they hunted deer, raccoon, otter, and birds. Creeping patiently along the rivers and lakes, they speared fish and netted turtles. On the fertile soil around their villages, they cultivated crops of maize (corn), beans, squash, and pumpkins.

It was inevitable that Europeans would one day discover this seeming paradise. Soon after 1500, Spanish navigators began steering their ships along the Georgia coast. Hardy Spanish adventurers returned to this region in 1539. Marching inland from the Gulf of Mexico, six hundred soldiers under the command of Hernando De Soto set out to find fabulous cities of gold.

Historians believe that in March of 1540, De Soto and his men crossed the Ochlockonee River and entered what is now southwestern Georgia. Seated on horseback, their helmets and metal armor shining in the sunlight, these *conquistadores* must have impressed the native people they encountered. At the end of April 1540, De Soto's expedition rafted across the Savannah River not far from present-day Augusta. Circling north and west, the Spaniards' hopeless quest for gold continued until De Soto died of fever in 1542.

THE SPANISH MISSIONS

During the next two centuries, Spain, France, and England all made claims upon the Georgia region. King Philip II of Spain sent Pedro Menéndez de Avilés with fifteen hundred soldiers to prevent French claims in the area by establishing forts along the Atlantic coast. The first of these forts was constructed in 1565 where St. Augustine, Florida stands today. A second was built just to the north, on St. Catherines Island, in 1566. Soon, the crack of biting axes and the crash of falling trees signaled the establishment of military posts on Cumberland, St. Simons, and Sapelo islands as well. The Spaniards allied themselves with a friendly Indian chief named Guale (pronounced "Wallie").

British pirate Edward Teach, better known as Blackbeard, attacked ships along the Georgia, Carolina, and Virginia coasts during the early 1700s.

Gradually, the entire coastal area became known as the Guale District, the first Spanish name for the Georgia region.

Deeply religious, the Spanish founded Jesuit and, later, Franciscan churches wherever they settled. In time, the ringing of mission bells brought many converted Indians to Catholic worship. A religious catechism translated into the Guale Indian language by Friar Domingo Augustin is believed to be the first book written in what is now the United States.

Other, less peaceful newcomers took advantage of the crooked waterways and snug harbors of the Georgia coast. From secret hiding places, French and English pirates sprang forth to raid Spanish galleons carrying golden treasures home from Mexico and Peru. English explorer Sir Francis Drake plundered the Spanish missions along the Georgia coast in the late 1500s. About a century later, bloodthirsty pirate Edward Teach, better known as Blackbeard, lurked about the region. Even today, legends persist

that pirate treasures lie buried in the forests of Georgia's
Blackbeard Island.

STRUGGLE FOR THE LAND

Spanish influence in the Georgia region continued to weaken
toward the end of the 1600s. From their bases in the Mississippi
River Valley, French scouting parties blazed trails along Georgia's
western frontier, while adventurous English traders from the
Carolina settlements canoed across the Savannah River. Attacks
by English-allied Indians wiped out most of the Spanish mission
settlements in the early 1680s. The surviving Spaniards fled to
their St. Augustine, Florida stronghold. Provided with weapons
and incited on all sides by the French, English, and Spanish,
Indian war parties kept the region in a state of constant
restlessness.

The encroaching English colonists of South Carolina proved to
be the most bothersome to the Indians. In 1715, war parties
organized by Creek chief Emperor Brim carried out a bloody
massacre of English settlements. As the Indians neared the gates of
Charleston (then called Charles Town), South Carolina, the
English banded fearfully together. United, they drove Emperor
Brim and his warriors back into the Georgia wilderness. In the
wake of the near destruction of their colony, however, South
Carolinians called on British King George I for military protection.

OGLETHORPE'S NOBLE EXPERIMENT

In England, grave problems of unemployment required the
more immediate attention of the king. Beggars drifted from town
to city in a hopeless search for work. People unable to pay debts

In 1733, James Oglethorpe (above) and 114 British colonists arrived at the spot that would become the city of Savannah (right).

were often thrown into filthy prisons. A government inquiry headed by a member of Parliament named James Edward Oglethorpe revealed the horrible suffering of these debtors. While reforms freed many unfortunate people from jail, Oglethorpe searched for a permanent means of providing England's poor people with work.

In the summer of 1730, Oglethorpe and twenty other prominent men sent a petition to King George II asking for a charter of land. The settlement of an American province to be called Georgia, in honor of the king, would offer unemployed English citizens an opportunity to begin new lives. Parliament disliked the idea of creating Georgia as a debtor's colony, and rejected Oglethorpe's plan. King George II, however, realized that a new colony would help stimulate trade and serve as a buffer between South Carolina and Spanish-held Florida. On June 9, 1732, he granted a charter for a corporation called "The Trustee for Establishing the Colony of Georgia in America."

The British people enthusiastically supported the project with money and supplies. Oglethorpe carefully selected Georgia's first immigrants from the hundreds that applied. The October 30, 1732 edition of the London newspaper the *Monthly Intelligencer*

After meeting with Oglethorpe, Yamacraw chief Tomochichi agreed to allow the British to establish a colony at Yamacraw Bluff along the Savannah River.

included the following notice: "The *Ann* galley, above 200 tons, is on the point of sailing . . . for the new Colony of Georgia, with thirty-five families, consisting of carpenters, bricklayers, farmers, etc., who take all proper instruments (such as hatchets, hammers, saws, shovels, spades, hoes, grindstones, and others). . . . James Oglethorpe, Esquire, one of the Trustees, goes with them to see them settled."

THE FOUNDING OF THE GEORGIA COLONY

A rough, two-month voyage across the Atlantic brought the *Ann* and its 114 passengers to anchor at Beaufort, South Carolina. Leaving the others behind, Oglethorpe set out to find a suitable spot for settlement. With his guide, Colonel William Bull, he rowed a small boat eighteen miles (twenty-nine kilometers) up the Savannah River. Standing on a high bluff, a group of Yamacraw Indians greeted him. Mary Musgrove, the half-Indian wife of a local trader, stepped forward to act as an interpreter. The *mico* (chief) of these natives, an aged warrior named Tomochichi, welcomed the idea of a peaceful colonial settlement among his people.

31

Among Georgia's earliest settlers were a group of Lutheran Salzburgers who left their homeland in 1734 (right) in order to escape religious persecution.

Before long, Oglethorpe had brought his little band of colonists to a clearing among the pines of Yamacraw Bluff. On February 12, 1733, celebrated thereafter as Georgia Day, they pitched tents and prayed for blessings on their new home. In these woods beside the river, Oglethorpe carefully laid out the street design for the town of Savannah.

England's unemployed failed to swarm to the shores of the Savannah River as Oglethorpe had envisioned. Fewer than two thousand charity cases ever reached the Georgia colony. During its early years, however, other settlers braved the long ocean voyage at their own expense.

A group of Lutherans from Salzburg in Austria journeyed to Georgia in search of religious freedom in 1734. The trustees of this group hoped to establish a silk industry in Georgia. At a community called Red Bluff, about twenty-five miles (forty kilometers) north of Savannah, the industrious Salzburgers planted mulberry trees and tended the silkworms that fed upon their leaves. On the colony's southern frontier on the Altamaha River, a group of Scottish Highlanders founded the town of Darien. By 1740, boats had also brought parties of Germans, Swiss, Piedmont Italians, Jews, and Welshmen up the Savannah River.

GENERAL OGLETHORPE

Threats of Spanish invasion from the south remained a constant worry. Using his skills as a veteran soldier, Oglethorpe supervised the construction of a series of forts along the coastal islands. Fort Frederica on St. Simons Island proved the strongest of these stockades. As commander of Georgia's militia, Oglethorpe felt ready when war finally erupted between England and Spain in November 1739. Oglethorpe struck first, marching his small army into Florida in 1740 and laying seige to St. Augustine. Disease and discontent among his troops, however, forced him to retreat after a few months. Then, in July 1742, scouts on St. Simons Island spied on the horizon the masts of some fifty Spanish ships. A vengeful Spanish army of 2,800 men soon trudged across St. Simons' beaches. Though Oglethorpe's defending force barely numbered 650, he remained confident. "I believe," he had written earlier, "that one of us is as good as ten of them."

Georgia's volunteer soldiers proved their worth on July 7, 1742. They skirmished with the enemy back and forth among the island's forest pines. Flushed with a false sense of victory, one force of Spaniards paused to rest beside a grassy marsh. Stacking their muskets, they prepared fires for their noonday meals. A detachment of hidden Highlanders lay waiting for just such an opportunity. The Scots suddenly poured forth a volley that sent

the enemy running helter-skelter. The defeat of the Spanish at this Battle of Bloody Marsh proved to be very important to Georgia's future. Tricked and disheartened, the Spanish eventually gave up their claim to the entire Georgia region.

Feeling that his greatest duty to the colony was at an end, General Oglethorpe sailed back to England in 1743, never to return. No one would dispute that his ten years of military supervision and faithful colonial service assure him the title the "Father of Georgia."

Among the original regulations set up by the Georgia trustees were bans on the private ownership of land and the purchase of black slaves. These laws proved so unpopular with Georgians that many of them abandoned the colony. The eventual offer of free land to immigrants who paid their own way across the Atlantic helped bolster settlement. But these new "adventurers" soon demanded slaves so that they could be gentlemen planters like their South Carolina neighbors.

Finally, in 1750, the trustees relented and allowed slave trade in Georgia. On June 23, 1752, they surrendered the administration of the colony altogether, returning the corporate charter to the Crown. Oglethorpe's vision of utopia reached its end as King George II took direct control of the colony.

GEORGIA AS A ROYAL COLONY

With the introduction of slavery, Georgia suddenly bustled with renewed settlement. In 1752, only about two thousand whites lived in Georgia, but already they possessed over one thousand slaves. Many Georgians eagerly laid out plantations along the river deltas and on the coastal islands. In these marshlands, their slaves waded up to their knees and bent beneath the broiling sun to plant their masters' rice crops. Wheat, corn, peas, and indigo also proved to be suited to the land.

Stories of Georgia's widening opportunities spread. Eager settlers traveling down from Virginia introduced the cultivation of tobacco. Scotch-Irish immigrants, Carolinian colonists, and even New Englanders arrived to develop the fertile lands that Georgia's royal governors awarded so cheaply. As a result of its defeat in the French and Indian War in 1763, France ceased to be a threat to the development of America's southeastern region. Pressured by an unstoppable wave of pioneers, Creek and Cherokee Indians surrendered great tracts of land in 1763 and 1773.

During its years of royal government, Georgia grew faster than any of Britain's other American colonies. By 1773, Georgia boasted fourteen hundred developed parcels of farmland. Most of these were small farms owned by inland, upcountry pioneers. On a few of Georgia's coastal plantations, however, landowners lived lives of wealth and ease.

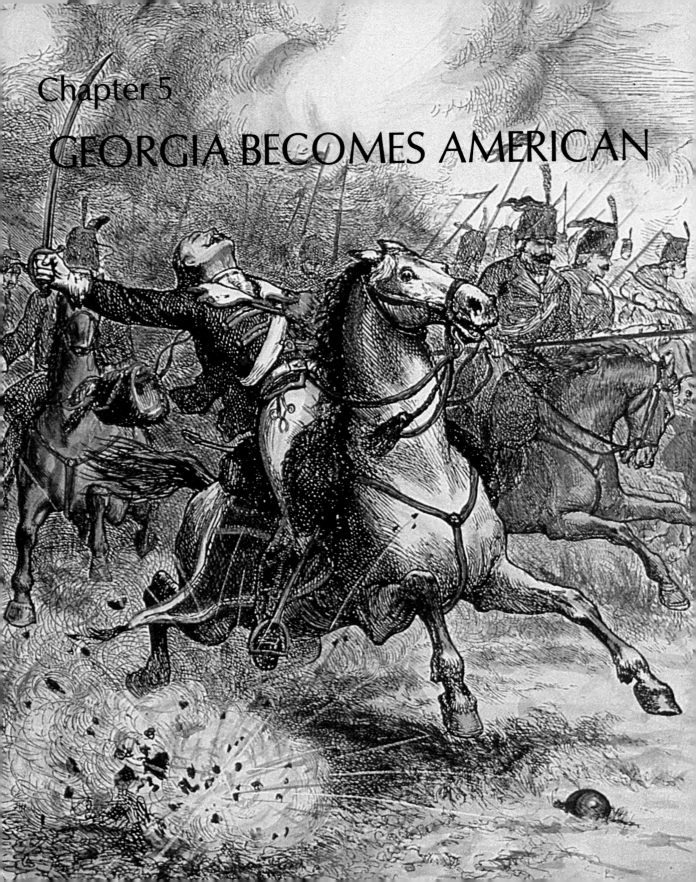

Chapter 5

GEORGIA BECOMES AMERICAN

GEORGIA BECOMES AMERICAN

"If we are no longer to be allowed the rights of Britons, we must be Americans," declared the September 6, 1769 edition of Savannah's *Georgia Gazette*. By that time, many Georgians had already guessed that their colony was on the road to revolution. The British victory in the French and Indian War had left Georgians free from the threat of foreign invasion and able to claim territory as far west as the Mississippi River. But the war's expense left England with a debt it expected America's colonists to help repay. Without consulting them, the British Parliament passed laws requiring Americans to pay import duties on such items as paper, glass, and tea.

Chanting "No taxation without representation!" citizens throughout the thirteen colonies protested these new taxes. At Tondee's Tavern, a popular Savannah meeting place, men who called themselves "Liberty Boys" or "Sons of Liberty" rallied to voice their anger. One of their resolutions declared, "His Majesty's subjects in America . . . are entitled to the same rights, privileges, and immunities with their fellow subjects in Great Britain." On the night of May 12, 1775, a group of Liberty Boys broke into the Savannah powder magazine and stole 500 pounds (227 kilograms) of gunpowder. On June 2, these Georgia rebels struck again. In defiance, they also spiked the twenty-one cannons being prepared for firing on King George III's birthday.

GEORGIA'S FIRST "CIVIL WAR"

Even at this date, however, a sizable percentage of Georgia's citizens remained faithful to the king. Georgia was, after all, only forty years old, and many of its settlers still remembered England fondly. The stubbornness of these Loyalists, or Tories, as they were called, led increasingly to violent confrontations. As open conflict loomed closer, many Georgia families found their feelings bitterly divided. James Habersham, for example, a wealthy partner in Georgia's oldest house of commerce, remained loyal to the king. Yet his three sons, Joseph, John, and James, all became radical patriots.

In January 1775, patriot delegates from throughout the colony met at Tondee's Tavern in Savannah. There they formed Georgia's first provincial congress. Meanwhile, patriots prepared themselves for war by forming military companies.

In March 1776, British warships sailed up the Savannah River in search of needed provisions. A brief clash along Savannah's wharves that became known as the Battle of the Riceboats marked Georgia's entry into the revolutionary war. Without the protection of British soldiers, Georgia's Loyalists now rose up to defend themselves. Some, calling themselves Florida Rangers, used British-garrisoned St. Augustine as a haven from which to conduct guerilla raids throughout southern Georgia.

On August 10, 1776, a messenger rode into Savannah carrying news of the signing of the Declaration of Independence. Thirteen cannons boomed in salute, as joyous citizens listened to public readings of Thomas Jefferson's bold words. Georgia's delegates in Philadelphia had been Lyman Hall, George Walton, and Button Gwinnett. By affixing their names to the documents, they achieved lasting fame as Georgia's "signers."

Button Gwinnett (left) and Lyman Hall (right) were two of the three Georgia delegates who signed the Declaration of Independence.

BRITISH ATTEMPTS TO CONQUER GEORGIA

The winter of 1778 saw British regiments marching inland from the Georgia seacoast. Near Sunbury, two hundred patriots under Colonel John McIntosh successfully defended Fort Morris. The patriot garrison at Savannah, however, experienced no such good fortune. British troops discovered a path through the surrounding swamps and breached the American lines. On December 29, 1778, Savannah fell into British hands.

During the months following this defeat, the struggle for northern Georgia intensified. A crucial engagement at Kettle Creek stopped British advances for a time. A disastrous battle for Americans at Briar Creek, however, gave the British continued hope of subduing the area.

Recognizing Georgia's desperate situation, George Washington sent General Benjamin Lincoln to take command of Continental (American) troops in the South. On October 9, 1779, Lincoln's men and an American-allied French fleet commanded by Count Charles Henri D'Estaing attempted to recapture Savannah. Polish Count Casimir Pulaski had come to America to fight for the cause of freedom. Leading a valiant cavalry charge into the face of withering British gunfire, Pulaski fell from his horse with a fatal wound.

Though the fight lasted only ninety minutes, it left the ground soaked with French and American blood. Of the four thousand men commanded by Count D'Estaing, a thousand had been wounded or killed. The battle for Savannah proved to be one of the deadliest fights since Bunker Hill.

Following this American defeat, the fate of Georgia hinged on an ugly, constant war between patriots and Tories. Parties of Tories roamed the north Georgia countryside destroying crops, burning barns, and murdering men, women, and children. Squads of vengeful patriots responded with equal violence.

Slowly, the tide of war began to favor those Georgians fighting for independence. In the spring of 1781, Continental soldiers led by "Light Horse" Harry Lee and Andrew Pickens arrived to help recapture Augusta. By 1782, after General Anthony Wayne arrived to take command of Georgia's troops, the war seemed all but over. On July 11, 1782, the triumphant entry of patriot soldiers into Savannah effectively marked the end of the fighting in Georgia. A year before the 1783 Treaty of Paris granted America her independence, victorious Georgians were hanging their guns above their mantels and returning to their plows in peace.

GEORGIA AS AN AMERICAN STATE

Georgians embraced their hard-won independence with enthusiasm. As early as 1777, delegates had drafted the state's first constitution. That body of laws allowed the state assembly to elect John Adam Treutlen as Georgia's first governor. In 1787, Georgia delegates William Few and Abraham Baldwin joined America's

A typical Georgia pioneer cabin of the late 1700s or early 1800s

other "Founding Fathers" in signing the United States Constitution. Georgia became the fourth state to ratify it on January 2, 1788.

Fully one half of the private property in Georgia had been destroyed in the revolutionary war. To encourage resettlement, the state government awarded free land grants of as much as 1,000 acres (404.7 hectares) to war veterans and their families. Offers of cheap land enticed immigrants from other states, as well as from Europe. Some "squatters," without paying for land, simply cleared themselves plots in the wilderness and claimed them as their own.

As old trading posts sprouted into villages and laborers cut the Indian trails into wider roads, Georgians demanded other signs of civilization. Elementary schools began to be established by farmers who understood the value of education. Children of various ages jammed into one-room log cabins with dirt floors. These humble places of learning came to be known as Georgia's Old Field Schools.

The cotton gin, which revolutionized the cotton industry in the South, was invented by Eli Whitney during his visit to a Savannah plantation in 1793.

Georgia's call for qualified teachers attracted Eli Whitney southward from Connecticut in 1793. Before taking up his duties as a tutor, the clever young man visited Mulberry Grove, a plantation just upriver from Savannah. There he learned about the cultivation of cotton. Although short-staple cotton grew well throughout the region, the difficulty of hand picking the clinging seeds from the cotton fiber made the crop unprofitable.

Encouraged by his hostess, the widow of war hero General Nathanael Greene, Whitney set out to find a solution to the problem. Within a few weeks, he had created a model of a simple engine whose rollers, teeth, and brushes made cotton cleaning easy. Whitney's cotton gin caused a remarkable transformation throughout the South. Georgians especially benefited from his invention. In 1791, the state's cotton growers produced only 1,000 bales of cotton. Within ten years, that figure had risen to 20,000 bales. By 1826, a stunning annual production of 150,000 bales made Georgia the largest cotton grower in the world.

THE YAZOO LAND FRAUD

"The hellish fraud of that infernal crew of speculators" is what the *Augusta Chronicle* called the Yazoo Act of 1795. The prospect of cheaply obtaining new lands on which to plant valuable cotton crops filled some greedy Georgians with dreams of wealth. Forming land companies, these schemers bribed state legislators to pass the Yazoo Act. The act awarded the speculators about 50 million acres (20.2 million hectares) of undeveloped, state-owned western territory at the ridiculously low price of $500,000. In return, many of the legislators were given stock in the land companies.

When the swindle became common knowledge, outraged Georgians turned the crooked legislators out of office. The act was repealed in 1796. Soon after, the government instituted a lottery system to distribute public lands more fairly.

THE TRAIL OF TEARS

Investors in the Yazoo scheme became involved in a legal tangle that lasted for years. Finally, in 1802, the federal government agreed to handle these claims in exchange for control of the land. Georgia ceded the Yazoo lands, as well as all Georgia-owned territory west of the Chattahoochee River, to the United States. The Yazoo territory subsequently became the states of Alabama and Mississippi. As a part of the agreement, the United States undertook the removal of the Creek and Cherokee Indians still remaining in Georgia.

During the fifty years following the American Revolution, these Indians clung stubbornly to what remained of their homeland. In 1825, Georgia's Creek were forced to sign a treaty at Indian

Sequoya (left) devised an alphabet that enabled the Cherokee to read and write in their own language. Soon, his writing system was being used to record Cherokee history and publish Cherokee newspapers and books (right).

Springs surrendering the last of their lands. Reluctantly, they relocated across the Mississippi River in the wilds of Arkansas.

After that, the only Indians remaining in Georgia were Cherokee living in the northwest corner of the state. These people, having adopted the ways of whites, had become successful farmers and even slaveholders. They organized an independent government, wrote a constitution, and established a capital city at New Echota. A statue erected in Calhoun memorializes perhaps the greatest of these Cherokee. After years of work, George Guess, better known by his Indian name Sequoya, devised a Cherokee alphabet containing eighty-six characters. This invention enabled

In 1838, the federal government forced the Cherokee to leave Georgia and begin a grueling westward journey that became known as the "Trail of Tears."

the Cherokee people to read and write in their own language. In 1828, the bilingual Cherokee newspaper the *Cherokee Phoenix* began publication.

The Cherokee of the hill country enjoyed peace and prosperity until 1828. Then, gold was discovered near the town of Dahlonega. As the news spread, miners suddenly flooded into the area, beginning America's first gold rush. To preserve their property, the Cherokee hired lawyers. They took their legal battle all the way to the United States Supreme Court. In the end, however, the United States refused to recognize the rights of the Cherokee people.

In June of 1838, federal troops began rounding up the Cherokee. They herded, often at gunpoint, fourteen thousand shocked and saddened Cherokee westward on foot to new lands in Oklahoma. The 1,000-mile (1,609-kilometer) journey lasted six months. The difficult terrain and harsh weather killed as many as four thousand Indian men, women, and children. The survivors called the path they had traveled *Nunna-da-ul-tsun-yi,* meaning "the place where they cried."

Chapter 6

SECESSION AND WAR

SECESSION AND WAR

All I want in this creation,
Is a pretty little wife and a big plantation,
Way down yonder in the Cherokee Nation.

Loudly singing this popular folk song, hopeful settlers poured into northwest Georgia during the 1830s. The acquisition of the Cherokee lands stretched the state's borders to essentially their present-day limits. Although the Dahlonega gold rush supplied enough gold to support a federal mint in that town, it was the state's "cotton rush" that gave Georgia landowners their greatest chance for fortune.

The rich lands across the middle of the state came to be known as the "Cotton Belt." Macon, established in 1823, grew into a thriving town that within five years was shipping nearly forty thousand bags of cotton down the Ocmulgee River. On the Chattahoochee River, pioneers erected a trading post in 1828 that grew into the frontier town of Columbus.

THE TRANSPORT OF COTTON

Cotton growers sought fast and easy methods to get their crops to market. From the interior regions, mule drivers guided wagons over crude roads. At river landings, laborers transferred the 250-pound (113-kilogram) cotton bags onto flat-bottomed boats

The advent of the steamboat in the 1820s improved Georgia's already thriving cotton trade.

called "cotton boxes" or "cotton flats." Boatmen guided their cargos downriver to the cotton exchanges of Savannah and Brunswick.

The introduction of the steamboat greatly improved Georgia's system of river transportation and hastened settlement. Since the state contained so many navigable rivers, steamboats proved enormously popular and practical. Belching black smoke and piled high with cotton, some seventy different steamboats plied the waters of the Savannah River between 1820 and 1865. At such growing settlements as Albany and Bainbridge on the Flint River, Georgians rushed excitedly to the river's edge at the sound of an approaching steamboat whistle.

The advent of steam-engine trains also dramatically changed the face of Georgia. Workers began laying track westward from Augusta to Union Point in 1833. By 1860, an impressive total of 1,226 miles (1,972 kilometers) of track crisscrossed the state.

The fever to build railroads in Georgia resulted in the birth of one extremely important town. Starting in Chattanooga, Tennessee, the Western & Atlantic Railroad wound southward through Blue Ridge forests and rolling farmland. Originally, only a rural post office existed where this track ended, twenty-five miles (forty kilometers) south of the Chattahoochee River. When three other rail lines also made that spot their junction, the growing settlement of Terminus changed its name to Marthasville.

In 1845, this boomtown changed its name again, taking the feminine form of the word *Atlantic*. Within the next fifteen years, the city of Atlanta became the hub of not only Georgia's railroad traffic, but of the entire South.

THE RULE OF KING COTTON

The growing importance of cotton production brought with it an increased dependence on slavery. Wealthy southern planters needed field laborers to plant and pick their enormous crops. Although Georgia's slave population in 1800 numbered fewer than 60,000, by 1860 that figure had jumped to 460,000. A healthy field hand could fetch as much as eighteen hundred dollars on the Georgia slave market in 1860. By that time, Georgians owned $400 million in slave property, an amount that represented half of the total wealth of the state.

To varying degrees, Georgia's plantations functioned like self-sufficient villages. Fanny Kemble Butler revealed that her husband's Butler Island plantation work force included "a gang . . . of coopers, of blacksmiths, of bricklayers, of carpenters, all well acquainted with their peculiar trades." Plantation life typically revolved around the "big house," where the domestic work of black servants, seamstresses, and cooks allowed the master and his family to live in gracious comfort. These stately mansions, with their whitewashed columns and broad porches, came to symbolize the antebellum (pre-Civil War) South of the 1840s and 1850s.

Most Georgians, however, did not share the lifestyle of the planter aristocracy. According to the 1860 census, three-fifths of the farmers in the state owned no slaves. These hardworking yeoman farmers raised cattle and grains as well as cotton. They

Antebellum structures such as this plantation house in Washington (left) and the Old Cotton Exchange Building in Savannah (above) serve as reminders of the time when cotton was king in Georgia.

wore homespun clothes, enjoyed varied degrees of financial success, and remained thrifty, respectable, and proud. Georgia's poorest class of whites lived on a level barely better than that of plantation slaves.

SLAVERY AND SECESSION

Georgia's richest planters, who held political sway in the state, were fiercely determined to preserve their slaveholding way of life. In the industrial northern states, thousands of European immigrants provided a cheap labor force for factory owners. Most northerners had no use for slavery, and many considered it a cruel and immoral institution. Through the 1850s, abolitionist (antislavery) northerners demanded that slavery be halted. In the face of these repeated attacks, many Georgians talked of removing their state from the Union. Radical southerners who were particularly pro-secession were given the name "fire-eaters." They fervently believed that each individual state had rights more important than the laws dictated by the federal government.

The slavery issue reached its final crisis with the presidential election of Abraham Lincoln in 1860. Many Georgians, fearing that Lincoln intended to restrict or abolish slavery, believed the moment for secession had arrived. In Congress, Georgia Senator Robert Toombs bitterly predicted, "The Union . . . is dissolved . . . Georgia is on the warpath!"

On January 19, 1861, by a vote of 208 to 89, a Georgia convention decided on an ordinance in favor of secession. By this act, Georgia became the fifth southern state to declare its independence from the Union. Two months later, Georgia joined the new Confederate States of America. Georgian Alexander H. Stephens agreed to serve as Confederate vice-president.

PREPARING FOR WAR

The April 1861 Confederate capture of Fort Sumter in the harbor of Charleston, South Carolina marked the start of the American Civil War. President Lincoln promptly called for federal troops to put down the southern rebellion and preserve the Union. Confederate Georgians embraced the coming conflict as a second noble war of independence. Volunteers eagerly joined state militias. Before the end of the war, Georgia would provide 120,000 soldiers to the Confederate army.

Georgians contributed to the war effort in other ways as well. At Governor Joseph E. Brown's urging, the state developed an impressive war industry. Augusta, Macon, Columbus, and Athens

Fort Pulaski, built to protect Savannah, fell to Union forces in 1862 after a two-day cannon barrage.

all operated factories that turned out guns, sabers, and other military supplies. One Augusta factory manufactured more gunpowder than any other in the Confederacy. Atlanta, of course, with its railroad network, functioned as the state's greatest munitions and supply center.

EARLY YANKEE THRUSTS

Employing the Union's vastly superior navy, Lincoln ordered a blockade of southern ports. In April 1862, federal gunboats landed blue-clad soldiers on Tybee Island. After a powerful, two-day cannon barrage, the Yankees pounded Fort Pulaski into submission. The Union recapture of Fort Pulaski effectively closed the port of Savannah. Thereafter, Georgians depended on daring blockade-runners to obtain rare and needed supplies. Sailing sleek schooners, these enterprising captains sped through the Union blockade at night. At neutral English ports, they traded cotton for coffee, tea, salt, and other valuable items.

Georgia's geographic location in the heart of the South protected the state from invasion during the war's first years. But

Clockwise from above left: The Battle of Chickamauga; the Battle of Atlanta; the evacuation of Atlanta; Confederate graves at Atlanta Cemetery

in September 1863, the Union army kicked at Georgia's very door. Yankee general William Rosecrans ordered his fifty-eight thousand men south across the Tennessee border. To meet this threat, General Braxton Bragg massed a force of sixty-six thousand Confederates. Along a winding creek called Chickamauga (meaning "River of Death" in an Indian language), the two armies clashed. For two days, the battle moved back and forth through tangled woods and underbrush. Finally, the beaten

Yankees retreated back to Chattanooga, Tennessee, pursued by Bragg's victorious rebels. Left behind on the bloody Chickamauga battlefield were some thirty-four thousand killed or wounded Americans.

THE FIGHT FOR ATLANTA

The Confederate seige of Chattanooga was broken in November 1863. The shaken southerners reeled backward into Georgia, where General Joseph Johnston hurried to reorganize them. The new commander of the Union forces in the West, William Tecumseh Sherman, received explicit orders: "Move against Johnston's army, break it up, and get into the interior of the enemy's country as far as you can."

Sherman's objective was Atlanta, 100 miles (161 kilometers) to the south. Through the spring of 1864, Sherman attempted repeatedly to circle around and destroy Johnston's Confederate army. Each time, at Dalton, Resaca, and New Hope Church, Johnston skillfully fought off the Union attacks before retreating. In frustration, General Sherman attempted a frontal assault at Kennesaw Mountain just north of Marietta. A bloody beating inflicted by entrenched rebel soldiers quickly persuaded Sherman to resume his more successful flanking movements.

July of 1864 found the two armies facing each other just six miles (nine kilometers) north of Atlanta. Through the summer months, a new Confederate commander, General John B. Hood, struck fiercely at the Yankees, only to meet defeat at Peachtree Creek, Decatur, and Ezra Church. The Union army's grip continued to tighten around Atlanta. A daily Yankee attack of artillery fire sent shells crashing among Atlanta's houses, and finally, the Confederates were forced to abandon the city.

Millen was one of the many towns destroyed by Sherman's troops during their "March to the Sea."

SHERMAN'S MARCH TO THE SEA

"I can . . . make Georgia howl!" General Sherman grimly predicted. By conducting a 300-mile (482.8-kilometer) march to Savannah, "smashing things to the sea," the Union general believed his army could destroy Georgia's will to fight. On November 15, 1864, Yankee soldiers set fire to Atlanta. The next day, Sherman and his sixty-two thousand men began their march across the state.

Split into two columns on four widely separated roads, the Union troops tramped along in high spirits. Lacking a regular supply line to feed his hungry men, Sherman ordered foraging parties to strip the countryside bare. These raiding "bummers" became the terror of those Georgians whose farms lay in their path. After taking everything of value, the Yankees often burned the farmhouses to the ground.

There was little the Confederates could do to stop this advancing army. At Madison, Eatonton, the capital at Milledgeville, Sandersville, Millen, and dozens of other towns, Sherman's army left its ruthless mark. On December 13, 1864, Fort

McAllister at the mouth of the Ogeechee River fell into Union hands. Following a brief siege, Sherman's hardy troops captured their final objective. On December 22, the jubilant general sent the news to President Lincoln. "I beg to present you as a Christmas Gift," he wrote, "the City of Savannah."

WAR'S END

The march of Sherman's army sliced the Confederacy in two. Behind it, 317 miles (510 kilometers) of railroad and $100-million-worth of property had been destroyed. The charred ruins of mills, factories, and farms filled the Georgia landscape across a path 60 miles (96.5 kilometers) wide and 300 miles (482.8 kilometers) long. As Union army surgeon J.C. Patton remarked, "We have laid a heavy hand on Georgia."

Sherman's army continued northward through the Carolinas. The Confederacy was tottering, and with the April 1865 surrender of General Robert E. Lee to General Ulysses S. Grant at Appomattox Court House in Virginia, it collapsed completely. President Jefferson Davis fled from the fallen Confederate capital of Richmond, Virginia. Union cavalry caught up with him at Irwinsville, Georgia on May 10, 1865, and placed him in chains. Union soldiers arrested Confederate vice-president Alexander Stephens at Liberty Hall, his Crawfordville estate. He and other leading Georgia secessionists were imprisoned for a time.

As the sound of gunfire ceased, it was obvious that few Georgians had survived the Civil War untouched by personal sorrow or economic hardship. Thousands of Georgian soldiers lay buried on the battlefields of Virginia and Tennessee. In Georgia itself, the destruction left behind by Sherman's soldiers left wounds upon the state that would require generations to heal.

Chapter 7

THE RISE OF MODERN GEORGIA

THE RISE OF MODERN GEORGIA

"With malice toward none, with charity for all." These words, uttered by President Lincoln, promised kind treatment of the conquered southern states. But the tragic assassination of Lincoln by John Wilkes Booth on April 15, 1865 destroyed the South's best hope of a smooth reunion with the North. Instead of following Lincoln's program, a powerful group of radical Republicans in Congress sought to punish the rebellious southern states. With the passage of the Reconstruction Acts, Congress sternly demanded that the southern states completely revise their governments.

When the southern states would not comply, Congress next declared martial law throughout the region. Georgia became part of the Third Military District, which also included Florida and Alabama. On March 30, 1867, General John Pope arrived in Atlanta. As the first of three military governors, Pope oversaw the activities of Georgia's new state government.

Georgia's years of Reconstruction were a time of political confusion and upheaval. Freed but uneducated slaves suddenly possessed the right to vote, while stubborn white Confederates unwilling to pledge allegiance to the United States were turned away from polling places. Packing traveling bags made from carpeting, dishonest Yankees hurried south to take advantage of this situation. These men, who became known as "carpetbaggers," sought to control the state government.

Southern blacks voting
for the first time

SLAVERY ABOLISHED

A major result of the war was the abolition of slavery. To help
former slaves adjust to their newfound freedom, the United States
government established the Freedmen's Bureau in 1865. In
Georgia, ex-slaves left their plantations and wandered to Macon,
Atlanta, Augusta, and Savannah by the thousands. The
Freedmen's Bureau aided these refugees with gifts of food,
clothing, and medicine. Bureau workers helped blacks find
employment and educational opportunities.

Confederate Georgians gradually recognized the futility of
resisting the Reconstruction demands of Congress. To regain
control of their state, they ratified the Fourteenth and Fifteenth
amendments to the United States Constitution. These amendments
granted American blacks citizenship and guaranteed them the
right to vote. On July 15, 1870, Georgia was at last readmitted into
the United States and allowed full congressional representation. In

Washington, Georgia senator Benjamin Harvey Hill announced hopefully: "There is no more Confederacy! We are back in the House of our Fathers, our Brothers are our companions, and we are at home to stay. . . ."

Many white Georgians remained very bitter, however. They resented the loss of their slave property, and refused to accept blacks as equals. These Georgians quickly determined to deny blacks a voice in state politics. By September 1868, Georgia Democrats were already voting Republicans out of public office. On election day of that year, riots broke out in Savannah, as whites openly turned blacks away from polling places. Elsewhere in Georgia, and throughout the South, a secret organization was gaining strength. Wearing white gowns and peaked hoods, members of the Ku Klux Klan galloped through the night. The beatings, murders, and other outrages inflicted by the Klansmen struck fear into the hearts of blacks.

TENANT FARMING

The end of slavery brought about the dismantling of Georgia's plantations. Blacks now expected wages for their work, but landowners possessed no money with which to pay them. Out of this predicament arose the tenant-farming system. Landowners rented out sections of their property to poor farmers, black and white alike. These tenants could seldom pay their rent in advance. Instead, they agreed to hand over a share of their crop at the end of each growing season.

Landowners often provided tools and mules for their "sharecroppers" to use. The food and clothing sharecroppers needed to survive through harvesttime could be bought at country stores that sold merchandise on credit. Since the landowners usually owned these stores as well, their power increased as their tenants grew more dependent.

OUT OF THE ASHES

The rebuilding of Georgia's economy required patience, energy, and enterprise. The burning of Atlanta by Sherman's army left standing only four hundred of the city's thirty-eight hundred houses and buildings. Almost immediately, Atlantans went to work. Laborers cleared the rubble, and carpenters hammered anew. Within a year, the population had risen to twenty thousand people, eight thousand higher than its prewar level. In 1877, the Georgia legislature voted to move the state capital permanently from Milledgeville to thriving Atlanta.

The bustling activity of Atlanta was, to a certain degree, reflected throughout the state. By 1867, the state had granted charters for ten new railroad lines. Along existing but ruined lines, workers restored tracks, water towers, and stations, and set trains running again. Georgia's businessmen established banks and founded textile, flour, and lumber mills.

Dade and other northwestern counties proved rich in coal deposits. In 1881, miners removed 100,000 tons (90,720 metric tons) of Georgia coal from the ground. North Georgia quarrymen cut blocks of granite and limestone for use by construction companies, and the state's numerous clay deposits formed the basis of brick and pottery industries.

In 1881, Atlantans held a World's Fair and Great International Cotton Exposition to advertise Georgia's progress. Thousands of visitors walked through twenty acres (eight hectares) of exhibits, including one that showed cotton "growing in the field in the morning, and picked, ginned, woven, cut, made into a suit, and

After being destroyed in the Civil War, Atlanta was rebuilt so quickly (left) that Atlantans chose the phoenix, the fabled bird that rose healthy from its own ashes, as the emblem for the city's insignia.

worn by night." Still, Georgia and other southern states lagged behind the tremendous industrialization of the North. Henry W. Grady, editor of the *Atlanta Constitution*, urged increased efforts to obtain industrial prosperity throughout the South. In a famous 1886 speech, Grady told a New York City audience, "The Old South rested everything on slavery and agriculture . . . The New South presents . . . a hundred farms for every plantation . . . and a diversified industry that meets the needs of this complex age." Grady's hopeful vision of a "New South" stimulated progress and pride among patriotic southerners.

THE VOICE OF THE FARMER

The Democratic party, which controlled Georgia politics, kept three men in power through the 1870s and 1880s. Wartime governor Joseph E. Brown and ex-Confederate generals Alfred H. Colquitt and John B. Gordon so dominated Georgia's governorship and Senate seats that they came to be called the "Bourbon Triumvirate." Their strong but conservative rule of the state often favored banking and business interests.

63

Georgia's many struggling farmers longed for greater political influence. In 1881, Thomas E. Watson, a McDuffie County lawyer, rose up and spoke for them. Georgia's farmers, he complained, suffered the "burden of unequal taxation," and "the impossibility of buying or selling except at other peoples' prices." Attacking the banks, he insisted, "This system is false and it shall die!"

Supported by a growing grassroots organization called the Farmers' Alliance, Watson won a seat in Congress in 1890. In Washington, Watson argued for reforms to help the nation's farmers. His greatest success occurred in 1893. The passage of his Rural Free Delivery Bill assured country farmers free mail delivery. Throughout the 1890s, Watson spoke and wrote on behalf of the rising People's party. For a time, this Populist movement challenged Democratic party policies. Gradually, Georgia's Democrats regained firm control of the state by making certain concessions to Georgia's white farmers, such as regulating railroad freight costs and preventing black Georgians from voting.

DAYS OF DEPRESSION

> I worked in the cotton mill all my life,
> I ain't got nothing but a barlow knife,
> It's a hard times, cotton mill girl,
> Hard times everywhere.

The lines of this Georgia folk song reflect the difficulties endured by wage earners throughout the state in the early 1900s. The new century had, however, begun on a hopeful note. In 1910, nearly two-thirds of the population remained involved in farming. Although cotton was still the major crop, county agents from the state College of Agriculture in Athens were encouraging the cultivation of other crops. By 1919, twelve million peach trees

graced the Upper Piedmont from Fort Valley to Floyd County.
Apple orchards, pecan groves, and watermelon patches
increasingly covered Georgia's southern landscape. Corn, tobacco,
sugarcane, and peanuts (sometimes called goobers) also thrived in
the state's warm climate. Georgia might have been saved from its
hardest times if it had relied even less on cotton. Around 1915, a
dreadful insect intent on ravaging cotton crops arrived from the
southwestern states. The Mexican boll weevil would lay its eggs
on a growing plant, and the hungry larvae that emerged would
devour the developing cotton bolls. In 1919, the Greene County
harvest amounted to 21,500 bales. By 1922, the harvest had
dropped to a disastrous 326 bales. Cotton production throughout
the state fell to about one-third of its highest level.

Georgia's struggling farmers were dealt an even heavier blow
when the New York stock market crash of 1929 cast the entire

Governor Eugene Talmadge, whose fiscal and racial conservatism appealed to Georgia's poor, white farmers and workers, is shown here making an impassioned speech against President Roosevelt's New Deal policies in 1935.

nation into an economic depression. During the early 1930s, thousands of farms failed and were abandoned. Some five hundred thousand victimized Georgians moved North to search for jobs.

Georgia's tough survivors looked to the state's government for help and leadership. Youthful governor Richard Russell, elected in 1930, reorganized the state government and trimmed its budget 20 percent before moving on to represent Georgia in the United States Senate for thirty-eight years. Perhaps the most colorful man to occupy the Georgia governor's seat during the 1930s was Eugene Talmadge. Talmadge's simple charm, explosive personality, and call for white supremacy over blacks excited struggling white farmers. Politically conservative, Talmadge called on the National Guard to break bloody textile-mill strikes in 1934, and warned his fellow citizens of the dangers of big government.

THE NEW DEAL AND WORLD WAR II

Needy Georgians, however, benefited from many new programs and reforms during the late 1930s. Under the guidance of

The "Little White House" (left) was the Warm Springs retreat where President Franklin Delano Roosevelt died on April 12, 1945.

President Franklin D. Roosevelt and the energetic leadership of governors E. D. Rivers and Ellis Arnall, soil conservation, housing construction, and other valuable public-works programs were implemented throughout the state. The surprise Japanese attack on Pearl Harbor on December 7, 1941 and the United States' subsequent entrance into World War II stirred Georgians to renewed activity.

Thousands of American soldiers received training at Fort Benning near Columbus, Fort Gordon near Augusta, and Fort Stewart near Savannah. Avionics experts at Bell Aircraft plant in Marietta designed, built, and tested bombers. The shipyards of Savannah and Brunswick launched more than a hundred of the cargo vessels known as "Liberty Ships." In 1944, Savannah dockworkers loaded more explosives for shipment to Europe than any other American port.

As World War II neared its conclusion with victory for the Allies, Americans mourned the death of their president. At Warm Springs in Meriwether County, Franklin D. Roosevelt kept an estate he called the "Little White House." It was while vacationing there that he died suddenly, on April 12, 1945.

During the civil-rights movement of the 1960s, Atlanta-born minister Martin Luther King, Jr. (second from left in first row of people) led nonviolent marches and demonstrations to end racial segregation and discrimination in America.

CIVIL RIGHTS

Georgia's reawakened sense of vitality continued into the years following the war. The founding of the Georgia Ports Authority in 1945, for example, sparked enough trade to turn Savannah into one of the liveliest ports in the nation. New scientific agricultural methods steadily increased farm yields. Industrial production rose as northern companies began to establish branches in the state and Georgians created more businesses for themselves.

As the tides of progress swept over the entire nation, America's blacks began demanding their civil rights. In Georgia, as in other southern states, blacks had suffered years of shameful treatment. A 1906 Atlanta race riot had left seventeen people dead in the streets. Between 1889 and 1930, mobs lynched (hanged without trial) at least 450 black Georgians for real or imagined crimes. In the late 1950s and early 1960s, blacks banded together throughout the Deep South. They refused to obey unfair state laws and challenged segregation practices that kept them separate from whites. The Reverend Martin Luther King, Jr., an Atlanta-born minister, became the leader in this movement for racial justice. In a famous 1963 speech given from the steps of the Lincoln Memorial in Washington, D.C., King proclaimed, "I have a dream that one day on the red hills of Georgia sons of former slaves and the sons of former slaveowners will be able to sit down together at the table of brotherhood."

Guided by King's philosophy of peaceful resistance, Georgia's blacks staged boycotts, marches, and sit-ins in their quest for full equality. Many resentful whites, however, violently resisted the idea of racial change. As whites rioted and clashed with demonstrating blacks, Georgia endured several years of turmoil. Gradually, however, blacks began to achieve their goals. A federal court ordered the University of Georgia to begin admitting black students in 1961. Slowly, other Georgia colleges and schools also ended segregation practices.

The passage by Congress of the Civil Rights Act of 1964 and the Voting Rights Act of 1965 guaranteed American blacks many of the educational, social, economic, and political opportunities they sought. In worldwide recognition for his role in this achievement, Martin Luther King, Jr. received the 1964 Nobel Peace Prize. When King was murdered by a sniper's bullet in Memphis, Tennessee on April 4, 1968, people across the nation mourned. In Atlanta, thousands of weeping people followed the simple wagon that carried the great leader to his burial place. Today, Dr. King's birthday, January 20, is celebrated as a national holiday.

MODERN GEORGIA

In time, racial tensions eased in Atlanta, partly because, as Mayor William B. Hartsfield suggested, it was a city "too busy to hate." Atlanta soon gained the reputation of being one of the

South's most racially progressive cities. In 1973, Maynard Jackson, Jr. was elected mayor of Atlanta, becoming the first black person to be elected mayor of a major southern city. Economic gains were being made as well. In the early 1970s, the city's skyline was altered by the additions of Peachtree Center, Colony Square, the Omni complex, and the World Congress Center. During this period of economic growth and increased commerce, the suburbs around Atlanta doubled in population and employment increased by 120 percent.

During the 1960s, Georgia had been governed by such conservatives as Lester Maddox, who before he became governor had refused blacks entrance into the Atlanta restaurant he owned. During the 1970 gubernatorial election, however, a peanut farmer from Plains stepped forward to present the views of more progressive Georgians. Triumphant at the polls, Jimmy Carter stated in his inaugural address, "I say to you quite frankly that the time for racial discrimination is over." As governor, Carter reorganized the state government, reducing the number of state agencies from three hundred to thirty.

Following his four-year term, Carter announced his ambitious plan to run for president of the United States. Completely unknown nationally, Carter began an incredible two-year campaign that ended with his election in 1976. As the thirty-ninth president of the United States, Carter brought his down-home Georgia lifestyle to the White House. He appointed Georgia congressman Andrew Young as United States ambassador to the United Nations. Many of Carter's closest advisors also came from Georgia. During his single term as president, Carter tackled many national and international problems. His greatest success occurred when he brought together Egyptian President Anwar El-Sadat and Israeli Prime Minister Menachem Begin. Their Camp David talks

Georgia native Jimmy Carter, shown here with his wife Rosalynn during his inaugural parade, served as president of the United States from 1977 to 1981.

led to an important peace treaty between their two countries.

Georgians delighted in the increased attention Jimmy Carter's presidency brought their state. Throughout the 1980s, strong local leadership continued to make Atlanta a city of international importance. Georgia's energetic governors traveled the nations of the world to encourage industrial development and investment in the state.

Problems remain to be solved, of course. In 1987, racial tensions flared in Forsyth County. Confrontations between Ku Klux Klan members and marching blacks made national headlines. In urban areas, many Georgians suffer the anguish of poverty and unemployment. The farming community has been faced with a crisis as well. Having borrowed money for equipment purchases and land expansion in the 1970s, farmers suddenly found themselves in debt when crop prices fell in the 1980s.

No easy solutions present themselves. But perhaps it ought to be remembered that since the days of Oglethorpe, Georgians have wrestled with hardship—and triumphed. Most likely, they will overcome today's difficulties and challenges as well.

Chapter 8

GOVERNMENT AND THE ECONOMY

GOVERNMENT AND THE ECONOMY

GOVERNMENT

The state government of Georgia is similar to the federal government in that it is divided into three branches. The legislative branch creates laws, the executive branch carries them out, and the judicial branch interprets them.

Georgia's legislature, called the General Assembly, consists of two separate chambers. The senate has 56 members; the house of representatives has 180 members. The legislature meets to design new laws, revise old laws, and assist the governor in planning the state budget. By electing their legislators to two-year terms, the voters of Georgia's 159 counties and 551 towns and cities assure themselves a voice in state affairs.

Every four years, Georgians elect a governor, the state's highest executive. According to the state constitution, no one may hold that office more than two terms in a row. As director of the state budget, the governor has control over state expenditures. As the state's chief law enforcer, he commands the state militia and police, and has the power to grant pardons. When legislative bills reach the governor's desk, he may sign them into law or veto them. The governor's veto can be overridden by a two-thirds vote in both houses of the legislature.

The judicial officers of the state interpret the laws through hearing court cases. The highest court is the state supreme court, whose seven justices are elected to six-year terms. The nine

Left: Berry College
in Rome
Above: The art museum
at the University of
Georgia in Athens

members of the court of appeals are also chosen by popular vote, as are the state's superior court judges. The governor appoints, with senate approval, only county and some city judges.

EDUCATION

Georgians currently spend more than $2.9 billion every year to educate their children. State-supported grade schools first began operating in 1872. Enrollment in school is mandatory for those between the ages of seven and fifteen.

Those who live just outside of Rome, Georgia speak proudly of the Berry Schools. In 1902, in a little schoolhouse built with her own money, Martha McChesney Berry began to teach the disadvantaged mountain children of the region. With loving care she nurtured the school, until at the time of her death in 1942, it consisted of a school for boys, a school for girls, and a four-year college. Today, some two thousand students continue to enjoy the facilities of Berry College's 28,000-acre (11,331-hectare) campus.

Georgia's state-supported universities and colleges include the University of Georgia in Athens, which in 1785 became the nation's first state-chartered university; and the Georgia Institute of Technology (Georgia Tech), which offers fine programs in engineering, architecture, and industrial management. Other state colleges and universities include Albany State College, Armstrong State College at Savannah, Augusta College, Columbus College, Georgia Southern College at Statesboro, Georgia State University at Atlanta, and West Georgia College at Carrollton. Georgia's most noted private university is Emory University in Atlanta. In 1977, Georgia financier Robert Woodruff gave $105 million to Emory, the largest single gift in the history of American philanthropy.

Other outstanding private institutions in Georgia include Atlanta University, founded originally as a center of learning for freed blacks after the Civil War; Clark College, also in Atlanta; Agnes Scott College in Decatur; and Wesleyan College and Mercer University, both in Macon.

THE ECONOMY

Georgia's civilian labor force numbers more than 2.7 million people. These workers earn an average annual wage of more than $17,000. However, a large number of farmers find themselves endangered by debt, and foreign competition has forced the closing of some factories and mills. Even so, Georgia's unemployment rate remains on par with the national average. The state's fertile soil, untapped natural resources, and many thriving industries still present workers with exciting opportunities.

AGRICULTURE

Georgia's fifty thousand farms cover 14 million acres (5.7 hectares). The state currently leads the nation in the

Georgia's fertile land provides the state with a variety of crops, including peanuts, pecans, soybeans, peaches, tobacco (left) and cotton (right).

production of peanuts and pecans. The more than 1.5 billion pounds (.68 billion kilograms) of peanuts harvested annually in Georgia represent about half of the peanuts grown in the United States. The yearly pecan crop accounts for a full third of the American market. Soybeans, tobacco, and wheat continue to emerge as valuable crops, and although cotton is no longer king in Georgia, it is still an important crop in the state.

Georgia is a leading producer of peaches. Georgia farmers also grow apples, watermelons, cantaloupes, grapes, pears, and blueberries. Among the vegetables grown in the state are sweet potatoes, cabbage, corn, snapbeans, and tomatoes.

Livestock represents a large portion of Georgia's agricultural output. About 1.7 million head of beef cattle graze Georgia farmlands. Hogs and dairy cows are being raised in increasing numbers. But the state's greatest agricultural contribution is its poultry industry. Georgia is the nation's leading producer of broilers and eggs. Every day, Georgia poultry farms produce and process more than 6.7 million pounds (3 million kilograms) of chickens and 1.1 million dozen-cartons of eggs.

Coca-Cola Company, headquartered in Atlanta, celebrated its hundredth anniversary in 1986 with several days of festivities.

MANUFACTURING

In 1886, an Atlanta druggist named John Styth Pemberton concocted a soft-drink formula in a simmering cookpot in his backyard. Today, Coca-Cola is consumed 250 million times a day in 145 countries. This enormous success easily makes Coca-Cola, still headquartered in Atlanta, Georgia's most famous corporation.

Many other types of products are made in Georgia. The state's most important manufacturing industry is the production of textiles, especially carpeting and cotton cloth. Cotton gins, fabric mills, and 285 floor-covering mills operate throughout the state. One-fourth of Georgia's factory workers are employed in textiles. The city of Dalton boasts that it is the "Carpet Capital of the World."

The manufacture of forest products also keeps many Georgians employed. Sixteen pulp mills turn out over 18,000 tons (16,330 metric tons) of paper and cardboard each day. The state's annual harvest of trees supports a huge lumber industry. The famed production of Georgia's gum naval stores provides the nation with 91 percent of its supply of rosin, turpentine, and pine oil.

Cellulose, a pine product used in cellophane and plastics, has given rise to a chemical industry centered around Augusta. The manufacture of electronic components is a growing industry in the state. Georgia's largest single employer is Lockheed Georgia Corporation in Marietta, which makes aircraft. General Motors, Milliken, West-Point Pepperell, and Bibb Manufacturing Company are also large employers.

NATURAL RESOURCES

In 1766, England's famous Wedgwood Pottery factory received a shipment of high-quality Georgia clay. Since that time, the clays, stones, and minerals of Georgia have been valued throughout the world.

Georgia's Fall Line Hills yield most of the United States' kaolin, a white, chalky clay used in the manufacture of paper, china, and paints. Fuller's earth, another clay product found in Georgia, is used in the processing and filtering of animal, vegetable, and mineral oils. Bauxite, the ore from which most aluminum is made, is mined in southwest Georgia.

For many years, architects and builders throughout the country have looked to Georgia for high-grade granite. Georgia granite was included in the United States Capitol building. Today, rich deposits in Elbert, Warren, Rockdale, and other north Georgia counties still provide the nation with granite blocks and gravel. Construction crews and sculptors sometimes travel to Georgia to find marble for use in buildings and monuments. A 3-mile- (4.8-kilometer-) wide belt of fine marble extends southward through Fannin, Gilmer, Pickens, and Cherokee counties. Murray County provides much of the world's talc and soapstone. Other valued minerals taken from the Georgia earth include feldspar, mica, limestone, barite, and ocher.

TRANSPORTATION AND COMMUNICATION

At Hartsfield Atlanta International Airport, jet planes take off and land constantly, like bees around a giant hive. In recent years, increased traffic has made it one of the busiest airports in the world. The many freeways and railroad tracks that lead into the city also testify that Atlanta has become the transportation center of the southeastern United States.

Because of its strategic location, people and products crisscross Georgia in ever-growing numbers. The state boasts a total of 128 private and commercial airfields, 5,468 miles (8,798 kilometers) of railroad track, and more than 100,000 miles (160,900 kilometers) of urban and rural roads. In recent years, Savannah has emerged as one of the busiest cargo ports in the South. Brunswick and St. Marys offer valuable seaport facilities, and river traffic still moves on the Savannah, Chattahoochee, and Flint rivers.

Currently, twenty-four Georgia television stations provide programming. The biggest name in Georgia broadcasting is that of Ted Turner. In 1976, Turner bought his first television station, WTBS, to provide free airtime for the professional baseball and basketball teams he owns, the Atlanta Braves and Atlanta Hawks. Today, cable stations of the Turner Broadcasting System, such as the Cable News Network (CNN), are viewed throughout the country.

Georgia's 310 radio stations provide listeners with everything from news, sports, and talk shows to rock, jazz, country-western, and classical music. Atlanta station WSB, established in 1922, was the South's first radio station. Of the state's twenty-nine daily newspapers, the *Atlanta Constitution* remains the most prestigious. Other widely read papers include the *Atlanta Journal*, the *Augusta Chronicle*, the *Columbus Enquirer*, and the *Savannah Morning News*.

Chapter 9

CULTURE
AND RECREATION

CULTURE AND RECREATION

It can be said that the deeds of Georgians are the blood that pulses through the heart of the state. The people of Georgia are proud of their heritage, which has produced a wealth of folk culture, literature, and music. Georgia's hardworking citizens also enjoy their well-earned leisure time. Professional and college sports teams, outdoor recreation, and the visual and performing arts offer state residents many opportunities for amusement.

FOLK CULTURE

"Okay, what are we going to have in this magazine?" asked Eliot Wigginton. In 1966, the young English teacher was searching for a way to excite the teenage students of Rabun Gap-Nacoochee School. The idea of creating a magazine, to be called *Foxfire*, seemed to interest them.

The first issue of *Foxfire* was a huge success. One article described superstitions that the students had gathered from their grandparents and local residents. Another listed country home remedies, such as "Carry a raw potato in your pocket to prevent rheumatism." Subsequent editions dealt with other facets of Georgia's rich folk culture. First edited into book form in 1972, and then expanded into an ongoing series, *Foxfire* became a well-known source from which to learn about such American folk arts and practices as log-cabin building, spinning, weaving, herbal medicine, and tanning animal hides.

Traditional folk arts such as quilting still thrive in Georgia.

From the Blue Ridge Mountains to the Okefenokee Swamp, pioneer arts and crafts are still alive in Georgia. At dozens of fairs and festivals, Georgians display and sell handcrafted baskets and carpentry items, as well as leather goods and canned preserves. The purchaser of a finely stitched, homemade Georgia quilt has without question obtained a valuable prize. The Fort Mountain Craft Village near Chatsworth and the Okefenokee Heritage Center in Waycross showcase full selections of Georgia folk crafts. In Tallulah Falls there is a craft store owned by a mountain arts cooperative. At the Agrirama in Tifton, tourists step back a hundred years in Georgia cultural history. A working farm and village, the Agrirama contains an old-fashioned gristmill, a sawmill, a cotton gin, and thirty-two other restored structures.

Among the Agrirama's main attractions are its musical presentations. The plink of a banjo and the scrape of bow on fiddle signal the start of many a Georgia folk melody. The lyrics of local square-dance songs are unusual and often amusing. One ditty, for example, goes:

> Jaybird died of the whoopin' cough,
> Bullfrog died of the colic.
> Jack came along with a fiddle on his back
> And asked 'em all to the frolic.

Georgia's bountiful musical tradition has been passed down from parent to child for generations. Originating from the Blue Ridge Mountains of North Georgia, such earthy tunes as "John Henry," "Cindy in the Summertime," and "Hand Me Down My Walking Cane" have become American folk standards. "Fa-so-la" singing, in which only four of the standard seven tones of the musical scale are used, is a type of traditional folk music unique to the North Georgia region.

Years ago, Georgia's slaves sang songs of hope and inspiration while working in the fields. Today, many of these lovely gospel melodies are still cherished by black church choirs.

LITERATURE

> "Howdy, Brer Rabbit," sez Brer Fox, sezee. "You look sorter stuck up dis mawnin'," sezee, en den he rolled on de groun', en laughed en laughed twel he couldn't laugh no mo'.
> —Joel Chandler Harris, "The Tar Baby"

As a young printer in the 1860s, Joel Chandler Harris listened to scraps of amusing animal stories told in the slave quarters of the Putnam County plantation where he worked. Years later, while writing for the *Atlanta Constitution*, Harris transformed and published these tales. Such stories as "The Briar Patch" and "The Tar Baby," narrated in slave dialect by an old character named Uncle Remus, became immediately popular. Today, the adventures of Brer Rabbit, Brer Fox, and Brer Bear are known to millions of American readers.

Though he is perhaps the most beloved of Georgia's writers, Harris followed in the footsteps of several other literary figures. Augustus Baldwin Longstreet's book *Georgia Scenes, Characters and Incidents*, published in 1835, wittily sketched life on the Georgia

An illustration from one of Joel Chandler Harris's Uncle Remus stories

frontier. In the 1860s, Charles Henry Smith became known for his humorous writings, which appeared in newspapers in the form of letters written in an illiterate dialect and signed "Bill Arp."

In Brunswick, a live oak known as the Lanier Oak still stands. It was while sitting under this tree in 1878 that Sidney Lanier wrote his famous lyrical poem "The Marshes of Glynn." In 1865, Lanier returned home to Macon after serving the Confederacy in the Civil War. While working as a musician and teacher in Georgia and Maryland, he began to write romantic and transcendental poetry. In his tender poem "Corn," he suggested reviving the southern economy by replacing cotton crops with corn. Today, Lake Sidney Lanier and Lanier County honor this favorite Georgia son.

While a professor at Atlanta University in the early 1900s, educator W.E.B. Du Bois wrote books and articles militantly urging equality and progress for his fellow blacks. In his best work, *The Souls of Black Folk*, he described Atlanta:

> South of the North, yet North of the
> South, lies the city of a hundred hills,
> Peering out of the shadows of the
> past into the promise of the future.

Throughout the world, the first response to a mention of Georgia is often "Oh yes, *Gone with The Wind*." After ten years' work on the manuscript, Margaret Mitchell published her Pulitzer Prizewinning novel in 1936. An epic romance set during the Civil War, the book describes the loves of heroine Scarlett O'Hara, as well as her struggle to hold onto Tara, her family's Georgia plantation. In 1939, Americans jammed theaters to see Vivien Leigh and Clark Gable star in the classic film version of the book. At present, *Gone With The Wind* has sold more than 8 million copies in forty different countries.

Another important Civil War novel set in Georgia is *Andersonville*, written by MacKinley Kantor. This 1956 Pulitzer Prizewinner is a fictionalized but accurate account of the horrors of the Confederacy's worst prison camp. Between 1864 and 1865, more than thirteen thousand of the fifty thousand Union soldiers imprisoned in the filthy, 27-acre (109-hectare) stockade died of exposure, starvation, and disease.

Georgian Erskine Caldwell wrote lurid tales of southern poverty and hardship. *Tobacco Road*, published in 1932, told the story of struggling sharecropper Jeeter Lester. Caldwell's *God's Little Acre* described a cotton weavers' strike.

The theme of loneliness is prevalent in the novel and stories of Columbus-born Carson McCullers. Her first novel, *The Heart is a Lonely Hunter*, focused on the lives of a deaf man and a teenage girl he befriends. *The Member of the Wedding* describes poignantly the coming of age of an imaginative but lonely young girl named Frankie. These and other works by McCullers sensitively portray the psychology of the South.

Milledgeville lays claim to another of Georgia's modern writers. It was while living there that Flannery O'Connor wrote her finest stories. In such collections as *A Good Man Is Hard to Find* and *Everything That Rises Must Converge*, she used violent or disturbed characters to depict the hypocrisy and cruelty that can exist in our society.

SPORTS

They called him the Georgia Peach. Before they had a major-league baseball team of their own, Georgians excitedly followed the exploits of Tyrus "Ty" Cobb, who grew up in the town of Royston. While playing for the Detroit Tigers (1906-26), and later for the Philadelphia Athletics (1926-28), Cobb set many records for batting and base stealing. His lifetime batting average of .367, his 5,863 hits, and his 1915 record of ninety-six stolen bases made Cobb an obvious choice when the Baseball Hall of Fame chose its first honorees in 1936.

In 1966, when the Braves moved from Milwaukee to Atlanta, another baseball great became a Georgia favorite. Henry "Hank" Aaron broke twenty-one baseball records during his twenty-three-year-long major-league career. It was at Atlanta-Fulton County Stadium, on April 8, 1974, that Aaron cracked his 715th home run to break Babe Ruth's incredible record of most home runs scored in a career.

Today, baseball fans still jam the stadium where Aaron performed his greatest triumphs. Under the guidance of team

Atlanta is home to the NBA Atlanta Hawks.

owner Ted Turner, the Braves keep alive hopes of pennant and
World Series glory. In the fall, groundskeepers lay down the lines
of a football field in Atlanta-Fulton County Stadium. The fans
who pack the seats during the football season come to root for the
Atlanta Falcons. In south Georgia, however, some fans prefer to
follow the activities of the Tampa Bay Buccaneers, or even the
Miami Dolphins.

College football is also popular in Georgia. In 1982, University
of Georgia running back Herschel Walker won the Heisman
Trophy, the highest award in college football. The Georgia
Bulldogs and the Georgia Tech Yellow Jackets are regularly
regarded as tough competitors. Every winter, college football
teams vie to play in Georgia's Peach Bowl.

At Omni Coliseum, the Atlanta Hawks basketball team has
caused plenty of thrills in recent years. During the 1986 play-offs,
the Hawks reached the NBA Eastern Conference semifinals.
Although the team lost to the Boston Celtics, the fine coaching of
Mike Fratello earned him the title NBA Coach of the Year.

Golf is another sport followed enthusiastically by Georgians.
Every April, the finest golfers in the world converge at the

Left: Fishing on the Okefenokee Swamp
Above: Hiking along the Appalachian Trail

Augusta National Golf Club for the Masters Golf Tournament, one of the sport's most important events. To win the Masters green coat is the dream of every professional golfer.

OUTDOOR RECREATION

The woods, lakes, and streams of Georgia's forty-five state parks cover 60,000 acres (24,282 hectares) throughout the state. In addition, the state has two national forests, Oconee National Forest in central Georgia; and Chattahoochee National Forest, which stretches 80 miles (129 kilometers) across north Georgia from Rabun County to Chattooga County.

Georgia's parks beckon visitors with numerous activities, including picnicking, camping, and boating. On the Chattahoochee and Chattooga rivers, adventurous types rent rubber rafts and enter rafting races. Hiking trails are numerous and include the great Appalachian Trail, which starts in Fannin County and winds for 2,100 miles (3,379 kilometers) all the way to Maine.

On private lands and designated areas, licensed hunters stalk quail, wild turkey, duck, and deer in season. Anglers catch trout

Cumberland Island, much of which has been set aside as a national seashore, has wild horses and the ruins of a mansion once owned by the Carnegie family.

in Georgia's northern mountain streams. Farther south, they reel in catfish, bass, bream, and shad. For those who prefer deep-sea fishing, Georgia's coastal waters yield redfish, tarpon, and mackerel, as well as other types of fish.

Georgia maintains more than twenty national wildlife preserves. Largest by far is the Okefenokee Wilderness Area, whose swamps cover large sections of Charlton and Ware counties. Off the coast, Wassaw, Ossabaw, Sapelo, Wolf, and Cumberland islands are set aside as wildlife sanctuaries.

THE ARTS

"All our knowledge has its origins in our perceptions," Italian artist Leonardo da Vinci once stated. Georgians take care to develop those perceptions at their many museums and theaters. The state's best-known art museum also happens to be one of its newest. Opened in 1983, Atlanta's High Museum of Art is lodged in a breathtaking white building designed by architect Richard Meier.

Emory University's Museum of Art and Archaeology, also in Atlanta, contains the largest collection of classical archaeological artifacts in the Southeast.

Across the state, other important art museums include the Marietta-Cobb Fine Arts Center, the Heritage Plaza Museum in Albany, the Georgia Museum of Arts in Athens, the Augusta-Richmond County Museum, and the Telfair Academy of Arts and Sciences in Savannah.

Atlanta offers a great deal for those who appreciate the performing arts. One can attend concerts by the award-winning Atlanta Symphony Orchestra at the Woodruff Arts Center. The center also houses the Alliance Theater Company, the Atlanta Opera, and the Atlanta Children's Theater. A dozen other Atlanta theaters, including the Moorish-style Fox Theatre, attract large audiences. The Atlanta Civic Center is used for summer musicals produced by the Theater of Stars company, as well as for performances by the Atlanta Ballet.

The performing arts thrive in other parts of the state as well. Today, the people of Columbus continue to view dance performances, musical shows, and plays in the Springer Opera House, a lovely Victorian building built by the town's residents in 1871. Little Toomsboro draws music-lovers from miles around to clap their hands and stamp their feet to the country, gospel and wiregrass music performed at the Swampland Opera House. Whatever a visitor's entertainment preference, he or she can surely find a pleasant way to spend a Georgia evening.

Chapter 10

HIGHLIGHTS OF THE PEACH STATE

HIGHLIGHTS OF THE PEACH STATE

From the craggy Blue Ridge Mountains to the sandy beaches of the coastal islands, Georgia's many natural and man-made sights fill travelers with excitement and wonder. Entering from the north and crisscrossing southward, a visitor to Georgia might wish to see some of the following attractions.

THE NORTH GEORGIA MOUNTAINS

From the peak of Brasstown Bald Mountain near Blairsville, one can see panoramic views of three states. A closer inspection of Georgia's northern mountains reveals numerous state parks in a region of overwhelming beauty. In northeast Georgia, Tugaloo State Park and Unicol State Park are two of the most frequently visited parks. Farther west, the camping and fishing facilities at Fort Mountain State Park, James H. Floyd State Park, and Red Top State Park are very popular.

Amicalola Falls State Park near Dawsonville boasts the state's highest waterfall. Perhaps more impressive is the gorge at Tallulah Falls. Dropping 2,000 feet (609.6 meters), it is believed to be the oldest natural gorge in North America. Vacationing Atlantans are often drawn to nearby Lake Lanier. In recent years, the Lake Lanier Islands have been developed as resorts that include amusement parks and water sports. Tourists desiring more stouthearted adventure can hang glide from the stony

Two of northern Georgia's loveliest natural sites are the gorge at Tallulah Falls (left) and Tugaloo State Park (above).

heights of Lookout Mountain, which extends from northwest Georgia into Tennessee.

The mountain region possesses many sites of historic or human interest. The town of Helen in White County began to attract visitors when it changed its architecture to resemble a Bavarian Alpine village, complete with cobblestone streets and German-style restaurants. Visitors especially enjoy Helen's springtime hot-air balloon races and fall Octoberfest. In the nearby town of Cleveland, "parents" of Cabbage Patch Kids can watch dolls be "born" at Baby Land General Hospital, where entrepreneur Xavier Roberts first developed the famous doll.

A visitor can still pan for gold in the picturesque town of Dahlonega, site of America's first gold rush. Remnants of

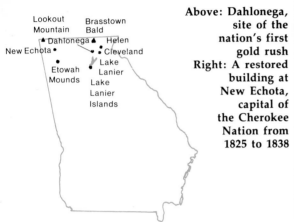

Above: Dahlonega, site of the nation's first gold rush Right: A restored building at New Echota, capital of the Cherokee Nation from 1825 to 1838

Georgia's Cherokee heritage are preserved at New Echota, once capital of the Cherokee Nation. The *Cherokee Phoenix* newspaper office, the court building, and a tavern stand restored among the ruins of the Indian settlement. About a half hour's drive to the south, the thousand-year-old Etowah Indian Mounds near Cartersville remind visitors that even the Cherokee were not the first Native Americans to live in the area.

THE BIG "A"

Behind us lay Atlanta, smoldering and in ruins,
the black smoke rising high in the air and hanging
like a pall over the ruined city.

With these words, General William T. Sherman described his army's fiery departure from Atlanta in 1864. Today, General

Left: Atlanta's
Center City Park
Above: A cafe at
Peachtree Center

Sherman and his Yankees would be astounded to see the city they destroyed. Zero Mile Post, the 1837 terminus of the Western & Atlantic Railroad, still marks the official center of Atlanta, but travelers are more likely to move about the city using MARTA, Atlanta's speedy, modern rapid transit system.

Atlanta combines big-city life with southern charm. Shopping is a joy at impressive Peachtree Center along Peachtree Street, or at any of the city's fabulous malls. After a rest at the fountain in Woodruff Park, a visitor might wish to browse the downtown Fairlie-Poplar district, which boasts a variety of architectural styles; or the Five Points area, the heart of Atlanta's financial district.

The gold leaf that covers the beautiful dome of the nearby State Capitol was mined in Dahlonega. The center of state government, the Capitol building also contains a state Museum of Science and Industry and a state Hall of Fame. The Capitol's dome shines down on historic Auburn Avenue, which runs several blocks to

The Martin Luther King, Jr. National Historic Site in Atlanta includes the birthplace, gravesite (right), and church of the late civil-rights leader, as well as the Martin Luther King, Jr. Center for Non-Violent Social Change.

the south. For a hundred years, Atlanta's industrious blacks have made successful lives for themselves along "Sweet Auburn." The birthplace of Martin Luther King, Jr., at 501 Auburn Avenue, is open to the public. At 407 Auburn Avenue stands the Ebenezer Baptist Church, where the Reverend King gave sermons. Next door, visitors can walk through the Freedom Hall Complex and pay respects at Dr. King's gravesite.

Astronomy buffs speak highly of the planetarium at Fernback Science Center. The Atlanta Zoo, located in Grant Park, possesses one of the largest reptile collections in the country. Also in Grant Park is the Cyclorama, a 50-foot- (15-meter-) high, 400-foot- (122-meter-) long cylindrical painting that depicts the 1864 Battle of Atlanta.

Swan House, a 1920s mansion, is now part of the Atlanta Historical Society.

At the Big Shanty Museum in Kennesaw just north of Atlanta, tourists can view the *General*. On April 12, 1862, James Andrews and twenty-one other Union spies stole the train engine *General* at Big Shanty station. The great locomotive chase that ensued proved one of the most exciting adventures of the Civil War.

Many houses of interest can be found in Atlanta and its environs. The Tullie Smith House at the Atlanta Historical Society dates back to 1835. The Wren's Nest, the quaint home of writer Joel Chandler Harris, is a popular tourist stop. The Lovejoy Plantation near Jonesboro is said to have been the inspiration for Tara in *Gone With the Wind*. Other communities within easy driving distance, such as Oxford, Covington, Newnan, and Roswell, feature many lovely homes constructed during Georgia's classic antebellum period.

Carved into the side of Stone Mountain is a relief depicting Confederate heroes Robert E. Lee, Stonewall Jackson, and Jefferson Davis.

THE PIEDMONT PLATEAU

Stone Mountain, standing starkly on the Piedmont Plateau, is famous for two reasons. Rising 825 feet (251 meters), it is the largest mass of granite in the world. But of even greater interest is that on the mountain's side, the carved, mounted figures of Confederate President Jefferson Davis and Generals Robert E. Lee and Thomas "Stonewall" Jackson form the world's largest bas-relief sculpture. Travelers who come to see the monument usually spend the day to enjoy the amusements of 3,200 acre (1,295-hectare) Stone Mountain Park.

Medical history was made in the Piedmont town of Jefferson on March 30, 1842. On that day, Dr. Crawford W. Long, operating on a patient's neck, became the first physician to use ether as an anesthesia. Today, visitors to Jefferson's Crawford W. Long Medical Museum can see some of his early anesthesia equipment and marvel at the true beginnings of painless surgery.

Two wars and the days of King Cotton have left their mark on the Piedmont region. Near Washington, amateur historians stalk the Kettle Creek battlefield searching for half-buried British and patriot musket balls and artifacts. Also near Washington is the Callaway Plantation, whose furnished buildings show what life was like during cotton's heyday. The Jarrell Plantation near Juliette, on the other hand, is a farm whose history spans from 1840 to 1940. Visitors can watch an old-fashioned blacksmith hammer horseshoes, or witness the more modern operation of a steam-powered mill.

Stretching southeast from Atlanta, the 1864 trail of Sherman's marchers can be traced across the Piedmont. Although few period houses still remain standing in the region, General Sherman spared the town of Madison, and many of its charming prewar homes remain intact. The Union army also passed through Milledgeville, Georgia's state capital from 1804 to 1868. The Old State Capitol building now graces part of the Georgia Military College campus. The Old Governor's Mansion, which Sherman used as a headquarters, was the home of ten Georgia governors.

First established by General Oglethorpe in 1735 as an important Indian trading post, the city of Augusta on the upper Savannah River continues to thrive today. Among the hundreds of historic houses that line its handsome streets are Meadow Garden, the home of Declaration of Independence signer George Walton. The boyhood home of President Woodrow Wilson is also open to the

An obelisk-shaped chimney is all that survives of Augusta's Confederate Powder Works, which supplied millions of pounds of gunpowder during the Civil War.

public. On Goodrich Street, a lonely chimney juts 176 feet (54 meters) into the sky to remind visitors where the Civil War's famous Confederate Powder Works once manufactured gunpowder.

In central Georgia, on the outskirts of Macon, Ocmulgee National Monument features Indian mounds that may date back eight thousand years. The mounds are part of the largest Indian archaeological restoration in the eastern United States. It seems curious that such a quiet, ancient place still exists beside Macon's smoking factories and busy city streets.

Although it is an industrial city, Macon's sixty thousand cherry trees make it a colorful place in springtime. Flower lovers also make a point of visiting Callaway Gardens at Pine Mountain on the Western Piedmont. Among the abundant natural beauties that visually enrich its 2,500 acres (1,011 hectares) of hills, meadows, lakes, and woodlands are hundreds of varieties of wildflowers. Those who love to eat peaches can satisfy their craving in the peach-growing region around Fort Valley. Orchard owners north of Perry invite travelers to pick the fruit themselves when it is in season.

Providence Canyon, located in the southwestern part of the state, is sometimes referred to as Georgia's "Little Grand Canyon."

THE GEORGIA PLAINS

Georgia's largest natural area is the plains region, noted for its vast, dry, pine forests and broad, flat farmlands. It is surprising, therefore, to discover Providence Canyon, called by Georgians the "Little Grand Canyon," near the town of Lumpkin in this region. Its huge gullies, caused by erosion, plunge 150 feet (46 meters). Many wildflowers grow from the canyon's brightly colored soils.

The town of Thomasville takes its flowers seriously. New, unnamed varieties of roses are cultivated at the Rose Test Gardens there. Rosebushes have been planted on almost every Thomasville lawn, and each April, a week-long Rose Festival is held in praise of the town's favorite flower.

At several places on the plains, time appears to have stood still. Westville, just outside of Lumpkin, is a re-creation of an 1850s

Georgia village. The pioneer days remain alive at its many active shops, as cobblers hammer shoes, carpenters split shingles, and candlemakers pour wax into candle molds.

Columbus has so many fountains that it is sometimes called the Fountain City. After visiting the town's Historic District, with its riverfront promenade and old ironworks, a visitor may want to take a Chattahoochee River cruise on the *Jubilee*, an authentic sternwheel riverboat.

The simple little crossroads town of Plains gained instant fame when Plains native Jimmy Carter became president of the United States in 1976. Unpretentious Plains residents happily point out to travelers President Carter's birthplace, as well as the secluded house where he lives presently. The Carter family peanut warehouse continues to operate near the center of town. Tourists in search of campaign mementos can purchase them at a gift shop run by Hugh Carter, the former president's cousin.

THE GEORGIA COAST

"America's greatest botanical garden" is the title naturalists rightly give the Okefenokee Swamp. With entrances at Fargo, Waycross, and Folkston, the Okefenokee Swamp Park offers wilderness walks through its peat bogs, and boat tours on its lily-decked waters. At every turn, the unusual plants and wildlife of the Okefenokee make photography an easy and delightful pastime.

The glorious vistas of Georgia's coastal islands also draw visitors throughout the year. Live oaks dripping Spanish moss, groves of spiky palmetto trees, sand dunes, and warm salt breezes fill vacationers with a sense of beauty and relaxation. Jekyll and St. Simons islands are open to the general public. Their beaches

Visitors to coastal Georgia can take a boat trip through the Okefenokee Swamp (left) or relax on one of Georgia's beautiful Golden Isles (above).

are perfect for swimming or getting a suntan. From 1886 to 1942, some of America's richest families used Jekyll Island as a private resort. The huge Jekyll Island Clubhouse still stands today, and daily tours are given of the luxurious "cottages" owned by such millionaires as the Rockefellers, Morgans, and Vanderbilts. On St. Simons Island, where some of Georgia's earliest history was made, one can visit the site of the 1742 Battle of Bloody Marsh or the ruins of old Fort Frederica.

On the mainland, the restored Hofwyl-Broadfield Plantation demonstrates how rice was produced in coastal Georgia before the Civil War. A stop at nearby Brunswick is a must for seafood connoisseurs. While sitting at a seaside restaurant, diners can watch the shrimp boats bring in the day's catch.

Savannah's many carefully preserved historic buildings include nineteenth-century row houses (left) and such architecturally significant buildings as the Owen-Thomas House (above), a Regency-style home built in 1822.

The centerpiece of coastal Georgia is the city of Savannah, considered by many to be one of the loveliest cities in the United States. Savannah's Historic Landmark District, the largest in the country, includes more than eleven hundred historically significant homes and buildings. The charming streets and squares, originally laid out by James Edward Oglethorpe, today bustle in living tribute to his memory. At the corner of Bull Street and Oglethorpe Avenue stands a lovely old house that was the birthplace of Juliette Gordon Low, who founded the Girl Scouts in 1912. The Trustee's Garden on East Broad Street, which dates back to Savannah's founding, was America's first public experimental garden.

Visitors to Savannah's Historic Waterfront District can browse in shops housed in the old cotton warehouses along River Street (left) or watch cargo ships move up and down the Savannah River (right).

Modern Savannah mixes elements of the past with the present. The cotton merchants' offices along Factor's Walk, with their ornate iron bridgeways, remind visitors of Savannah's antebellum era. The nine-block concourse of Riverfront Plaza, on the other hand, is a recent, multimillion-dollar restoration. Strollers can window-shop at the many art galleries and boutiques there, or stand at the water's edge and watch the cargo ships glide up and down the Savannah River.

For those who take the time to listen, Georgia is alive with a thousand songs illustrating its people, land, and history. If, as the state song says, "Just an old sweet song keeps Georgia on my mind," then the vividness and fascination of Georgia life surely will continue to influence Americans far into the future.

FACTS AT A GLANCE

GENERAL INFORMATION

Statehood: January 2, 1788, fourth state

Origin of Name: Named in honor of George II of England

State Capital: Atlanta

State Nickname: "Peach State," "Empire State of the South," "Cracker State," "Goober State" (all are unofficial nicknames)

State Flag: The state flag was adopted in 1956. One-third of the flag is a vertical bar of blue containing the state seal: an arch, representing the state constitution; three columns bearing the state motto "Wisdom, Justice, and Moderation"; and the date 1776, the year Georgia signed the Declaration of Independence. The battle flag of the Confederacy occupies the remaining two-thirds of the flag.

State Motto: "Wisdom, Justice, and Moderation"

State Bird: Brown thrasher

State Flower: Cherokee rose

State Wildflower: Azalea

State Tree: Live oak

State Insect: Honeybee

State Gem: Quartz

State Fossil: Shark tooth

State Fish: Largemouth bass

A covered bridge at Stone Mountain Park

State Song: "Georgia on my Mind," words by Stuart Gorrell, music by Hoagy Carmichael; adopted as the official state song in 1979:

> Melodies bring memories
> That linger in my heart
> Make me think of Georgia
> Why did we ever part?
>
> Some sweet day, when blossoms fall
> And all the world's a song
> I'll go back to Georgia
> 'Cause that's where I belong.
>
> Georgia, Georgia, the whole day through
> Just an old sweet song keeps Georgia on my mind.
> Georgia, Georgia, a song of you
> Comes as sweet and clear as moonlight through
> the pines.
>
> Other arms reach out to me
> Other eyes smile tenderly
> Still in peaceful dreams I see
> The road leads back to you.
>
> Georgia, Georgia, no peace I find
> Just an old sweet song keeps Georgia on my mind.

POPULATION

Population: 5,463,105, thirteenth among the states (1980 census); 5,976,000, eleventh among the states (1985 figures)

Population Density: 93 people per sq. mi. (36 people per km²)

Population Distribution: 62.4 percent of the people live in cities or towns; 37.6 percent of the people live in rural areas.

Atlanta	425,022
Columbus	169,441
Savannah	141,651
Macon	116,896
Albany	74,550
Augusta	47,532
Athens	42,549
Warner Robins	39,893
Valdosta	37,596
East Point	37,486

(Population figures according to 1980 census)

Population Growth: Georgia's population showed a small but steady increase from the first national census in 1790 to the mid-1900s. Although many Georgians migrated to other states in times of economic troubles—the Civil War in the 1860s, the boll weevil epidemic in the 1920s, and the Great Depression in the 1930s—the state's high birthrate offset the population shift. Since the 1960s, rapid industrial and commercial expansion in Georgia, as in other Sun Belt areas, has led to a significant population increase. Between 1970 and 1980, Georgia's population increased by 19.1 percent, compared to the national growth rate of 11.45 percent. Atlanta, ranked the nation's twenty-ninth largest city in population size in 1980, zoomed to the rank of fourteenth according to 1984 estimates.

Year	Population
1820	340,989
1840	691,392
1860	1,057,286
1880	1,542,180
1900	2,216,331
1920	2,895,832
1940	3,123,723
1950	3,444,578
1960	3,943,116
1970	4,589,575
1980	5,463,105

GEOGRAPHY

Borders: The states that border Georgia are Tennessee and North Carolina on the north, South Carolina on the northeast, Florida on the south, and Alabama on the west. The Atlantic Ocean determines Georgia's southeastern boundary.

Highest Point: Brasstown Bald Mountain (also known as Mount Enotah), 4,784 ft. (1,458 m)

Lowest Point: Sea level on the Atlantic coast

Greatest Distances: North to south—315 mi. (507 km)
East to west—250 mi. (402 km)

Area: 58,910 sq. mi. (152,583 km²)

Rank in Area Among the States: Twenty-first

Rivers: About half of Georgia's rivers and streams flow south and east into the Atlantic Ocean, including the Savannah, Ogeechee, Altamaha (formed by the Ocmulgee, Oconee and Ohoopee), Satilla, and St. Marys. The 350-mi.- (563-km-) long Savannah River, which forms the state's northeastern border, is Georgia's longest river. Georgia's west- and southwest-flowing rivers, including the Chattahoochee and Flint, travel through Alabama or Florida to reach the Gulf of Mexico. The Chattahoochee, some 330 mi. (531 km) long, is Georgia's second-longest river; it forms the state's southwestern border. Some streams of northwestern Georgia join the Tennessee River and reach the Gulf of Mexico by way of the Ohio and Mississippi rivers. The Suwannee River, popularized as "Swanee River" in Stephen Foster's song "Old Folks at Home," flows through the Okefenokee Swamp southwest across Florida and into the Gulf.

Lakes: Twenty artificial lakes or reservoirs have been created in Georgia by damming its rivers to provide irrigation and hydroelectric power. The largest is Clark Hill, a 38-mi- (61-km-) long reservoir on the Savannah River above Augusta. Other large man-made lakes are Hartwell, also on the Savannah; Sidney Lanier and Walter F. George on the Chattahoochee; Seminole on the Flint and Chattahoochee; Sinclair on the Oconee, and Allatoona on the Etowah River. Some seventy thousand smaller bodies of water are found throughout Georgia, including natural lakes in the north and southwest and many small ponds created by the United States Soil Conservation Service.

Topography: Georgia may be divided into three topographical regions or bands extending from east to west across the state: the northern mountains, the central Piedmont Plateau, and the southern coastal plain.
Georgia's northern mountain region, a part of the Appalachian Mountain range, occupies almost 2,000 sq. mi. (5,180 km²). It includes a portion of the Appalachian Plateau, in the extreme northwest corner of the state. Southwest of the plateau is an extension of the Appalachian Ridge and Valley Region. Long, parallel ridges separate broad valleys of rich farmland. Georgia's highest peaks, ranging from 2,000-5,000 ft. (610-1,524 m), are part of the Blue Ridge Mountains in the northeast corner of the state.
The Piedmont Plateau, extending from east to west across central Georgia, occupies nearly a third of the state. It is a region of gently rolling hills broken by a few high hills, ridges, and deep river valleys. The Piedmont Plateau is Georgia's most heavily populated area. It contains most of the state's large cities, industries,

Left: Ferns in Chattahoochee National Forest
Right: Rock City, a group of rock formations atop Lookout Mountain

and much of its richest farmland. The 100-mi.- (161-km-) long boundary between the Piedmont Plateau and the coastal plain is known as the Fall Line.

The coastal plain includes the entire southern half of Georgia, from the Fall Line to the Atlantic coast and the Florida border. Georgia's Atlantic coastline stretches 100 mi. (161 km) from the Savannah River in the north to the mouth of the St. Marys in the south. If all the bays, river mouths, and coastal islands were traced, however, the total distance would measure 2,344 mi. (3,772 km). Bogs and marshes follow the coastline. Okefenokee Swamp, the second-largest freshwater swamp in the United States, occupies Georgia's extreme southeast corner.

Climate: Georgia's climate is generally mild. The northern mountain region has cool summers and may have cold winters. The Piedmont and coastal areas experience warm, humid summers and short, mild winters. January temperatures average 39° F. (3.8° C) in the mountains, 44° F. (6.6° C) in the Piedmont, and 54° F. (12° C) on the coast. The average temperature in July ranges from 78° F. (25° C) in the north, to 80° F. (26.6° C) in the Piedmont, to 82° F. (27.7° C) on the coast. The highest recorded temperature in Georgia was 112° F. (44° C) at Louisville on July 24, 1952. The lowest recorded temperature in Georgia was -17° F. (-27° C) in Floyd County on January 27, 1940. Georgia's average annual precipitation is 49 in. (124.5 cm), with the heaviest rainfall (over 75 in./190.5 cm) occurring in the Blue Ridge area and the lightest (less than 45 in./114 cm) in the east-central area. Annual snowfall rarely exceeds 1 in. (2.5 cm). Tornadoes may occur in the northern mountains; hurricanes are a threat along the coast. In 1986, a record heat wave killed more than a dozen people, destroyed crops, and brought many farmers to the brink of bankruptcy.

NATURE

Trees: Beech, birch, buckeye, red cedar, chestnut, cypress, dogwood, gums (black, red, and sweet), hemlock, hickory, magnolia, maple, red and white oak, live oak, pecan, pines (longleaf, shortleaf, loblolly, slash, scrub, and white), wild plum, yellow poplar, sassafras, sycamore

Wild Plants: Camellia, daisy, hibiscus, honeysuckle, poinsettia, Cherokee rose, violet; flowering shrubs include chinaberry, elderberry, yellow jasmine, mountain laurel, quince, rhododendron, Spanish moss, marsh grasses

Animals: Bears, beavers, deer, foxes, mink, muskrats, opossums, rabbits, raccoons, squirrels, wildcats, alligators, frogs, salamanders, sea turtles, snakes

Birds: Blue jays, catbirds, doves, ducks, snowy egrets, grouse, marsh hens, white ibis, mockingbirds, sandhill pipers, quail, sparrows, towhees, brown thrashers, wood thrushes, wild turkeys, woodpeckers

Fish: Freshwater fish include bass, bream, catfish, eel, sunfish, mackerel, rainbow trout, and shad; in coastal waters are crabs, oysters, and shrimp.

GOVERNMENT

The government of Georgia, like that of the federal government, is divided into three branches—legislative, executive, and judicial. The state's legislative branch, the General Assembly, consists of two chambers. The senate has 56 members and the house of representatives has 180 members. Both senators and representatives are elected by the people to two-year terms. The General Assembly makes new laws, revises and rescinds old ones, and assists the governor in the preparation of the state budget.

The executive branch is headed by the governor, who administers the law. The governor is elected to a four-year term and may not serve more than two successive terms. The governor is director of the state budget and has control over expenditures. The governor is also the chief law enforcement officer of the state and the commander-in-chief of the state militia. He has the power to veto bills of the legislature. The legislature can override his veto with a two-thirds vote.

The judicial branch interprets laws and tries cases. The state has three kinds of courts: supreme, appellate, and trial. The highest court, the supreme court, has seven justices who are elected by the state's voters to six-year terms. The court of appeals has nine members, all of whom are elected by popular vote. Superior court judges are also elected by the people. County judges and some city judges are appointed by the governor, subject to senate approval.

Number of Counties: 159

U.S. Representatives: 10

Electoral Votes: 12

EDUCATION

Georgia has about 1,800 elementary and secondary public schools, with an enrollment of more than 1.1 million students. The state has 537 private schools, with an enrollment of 85,654 students.

Georgia's land yields a number of mineral products, including
kaolin (left) and marble (right).

Georgia has thirty-eight senior colleges and universities, twenty-three
community colleges, and thirty vocational-technical schools. Graduate studies are
available at sixteen public and thirteen private institutions. The University of
Georgia at Athens includes schools of medicine, law, pharmacy, veterinary
medicine, business, agriculture, education, journalism, and liberal arts. Georgia
Institute of Technology, a state school in Atlanta, offers courses in engineering,
architecture, and science. Other state colleges and universities include Georgia
State University at Atlanta, Albany State College, Augusta College, Columbus
College, Georgia Southern College at Statesboro, and West Georgia College at
Carrollton. Emory University in Atlanta is the state's largest private university.
Other private colleges and universities in Georgia include Morehouse College in
Atlanta; Agnes Scott College in Decatur; Clark College and Atlanta University,
both in Atlanta; Wesleyan College and Mercer University, both in Macon; and
Berry College in Rome.

ECONOMY AND INDUSTRY

Principal Products:
Agriculture: Peanuts, soybeans, pecans, cotton, pimento peppers, snap beans,
sweet potatoes, cabbage, corn, tomatoes, eggs, tobacco, peaches, cattle, poultry,
sugarcane, wheat, dairy products, hogs, apples, watermelons, cantaloupes, grapes,
pears, blueberries, plums
Manufacturing: Paper products, textiles, food products, chemical products,
lumber and wood products, transportation equipment, apparel, petroleum,
fabricated metals, printing, electrical and nonelectrical machinery
Natural Resources: Forests, bauxite, shellfish, fertile soils, clays, granite, marble,
feldspar, barite, gold, talc, sand, gravel, fuller's earth, limestone, mica, peat, slate

Business and Trade: The manufacture of textiles is Georgia's single-largest
industry. Georgia is a leading producer of carpeting and cotton cloth. Other
important industries include the manufacture of food products, including peanut,
fruit, and vegetable products; transportation equipment; chemical products,
including agricultural and industrial chemicals; paper products, including
newsprint, paperboard, and other grades of paper; and wood products, including

turpentine, rosin, pine oil, cellophane, rayon, plastics, lumber, and furniture. Among the state's largest employers are Coca-Cola, with its home office in Atlanta; and Lockheed Georgia Corporation, which makes aircraft in Marietta. General Motors, Milliken, West-Point Pepperell, and Bibb Manufacturing Company are also large employers.

Atlanta is an increasingly important convention and trade-show center. Each year, more than 10 million people use Georgia's state and national parks and forests, and tourists spend 7.6 billion dollars in the state.

Communication: Georgia has 29 daily and 143 weekly newspapers. One of the state's most important newspapers is the *Atlanta Constitution.* Other important newspapers include the *Atlanta Journal,* the *Augusta Chronicle* and *Augusta Herald,* the *Enquirer* and *Ledger* in Columbus, the *News* and *Telegraph* in Macon, and the *Morning News* and *Evening Press* in Savannah. Georgia has 310 radio stations and 24 television stations. One of these is TBS (Turner Broadcasting System), an independent television network owned by Ted Turner.

Transportation: Hartsfield Atlanta International Airport is at or near the top of the list of the world's busiest airports. Scheduled commercial air service is available at 9 other airports; a total of about 250 airports serve Georgia's general aviation needs. Savannah, Georgia's principal seaport, is among the nation's top ten general cargo ports. Brunswick and St. Marys are also important deepwater ports. Because of an extensive network of locks and dams, rivers play a significant role in Georgia's transportation system. River barges can reach inland as far as Augusta, 230 mi. (371 km) from the sea; and Columbus, 270 mi. (434 km) inland. Georgia has over 18,000 mi. (28,962 km) of federal and state highways and 1,219 mi. (1,961 km) of interstate highways. The state's two major railway systems have a combined network of 5,468 mi. (8,798 km) of track.

SOCIAL AND CULTURAL LIFE

Museums: Georgia has many notable museums and private galleries. Among the best known are the High Museum of Art, housed in the Robert W. Woodruff Arts Center in Atlanta; and the Telfair Academy of Arts and Sciences in Savannah. The Georgia Museum of Art in Athens, which was designated the official state art museum in 1982, includes permanent collections of nineteenth- and twentieth-century American paintings, and European, American, and Oriental prints and drawings. The Albany Museum of Art offers special collections of American and African Art. The Cyclorama in Atlanta is a 400 x 50 ft. (122 x 15 m) cylindrical painting depicting the Civil War's Battle of Atlanta. Macon has a Museum of Arts and Sciences and a Planetarium. The Atlanta Zoo, the state's largest, is located in Grant Park in Atlanta. In addition, Georgia has many specialized museums. The Uncle Remus Museum and Park in Eatonton recalls the slave-cabin setting of Joel Chandler Harris' "Uncle Remus" stories, which Harris began writing while living in this area. The Warner Robins Air Force Museum has outstanding historic and futuristic aviation displays. The Military Museum in Hinesville features weapons, uniforms, flags, and equipment from the Civil War to the present. The National

Auto racing, shown here at Lanier Raceway in Gainesville, is a popular sport in Georgia.

Infantry Museum is located at Fort Benning in Columbus. The Gold Museum in Dahlonega commemorates the nation's first major gold rush. The Crawford W. Long Museum in Jefferson is the site of the first operation in which ether was used as an anesthesia.

Libraries: Georgia's first library was established in Savannah in 1736. Today, Georgia has thirty-six regional and eleven county library systems, with holdings in excess of eight million volumes. The state's largest public library is the Atlanta-Fulton Public Library in Atlanta. The University of Georgia has the state's largest academic library. It includes large collections on the history of Georgia and the South. The Asa Griggs Candler Library at Emory University is noted for its large collections of works dealing with the Confederacy and the history of the Methodist church. The Georgia State Historical Society maintains its own library of Georgia historical works. The Carter Presidential Center in Atlanta houses the Jimmy Carter Library, which contains the presidential papers of the nation's thirty-ninth president. The Margaret Mitchell Library in Fayetteville has an extensive collection of works on the Civil War.

Performing Arts: The Atlanta Memorial Arts Building, part of the Robert W. Woodruff Arts Center, houses the Atlanta Symphony Orchestra, which performs classical music under the direction of Robert Shaw; the Alliance Theater in Atlanta, which is one of the nation's largest non-profit theaters and presents theatrical productions ranging from Shakespeare to Broadway musicals; the Atlanta Opera; and the Atlanta Children's Theater. Musicals and ballet are offered at the Atlanta Civic Center. Other prominent theaters in Atlanta include the Fox Theater, Nexus Theater, and the Academy Theater for Youth. Outside of Atlanta, the Theater in the Square in Marietta presents high-quality productions. The Columbus Symphony performs at the Three Arts Theater in Columbus. At Columbus College, musicals are presented on a continuous basis.

Sports and Recreation: In professional baseball, Atlanta is represented in the National League by the Atlanta Braves, who make their home in Atlanta-Fulton County Stadium. The Atlanta Falcons of the National Football League also play their home games there. The Atlanta Hawks of the National Basketball Association play in Omni Coliseum. The Augusta National Golf Course, one of the nation's most famous golf courses, is the site of the annual Masters Golf Tournament. Auto

117

racing is also a popular sport in Georgia. The Atlanta International Speedway in Hampton has two Grand National race events each year, plus many Indy-car races, motorcross races, and other motor-sport events.

Georgia has more than 100 mi. (161 km) of coastal beaches and 3,000 sq. mi. (7,770 km²) of mountain forests, many of which boast deep lakes and clear streams. More than twenty wildlife refuges in the state, including the Okefenokee National Wildlife Refuge, attract nature lovers. Plant lovers enjoy the Callaway Gardens near Pine Mountain and the Camellia Gardens of the American Camellia Society in Fort Valley. The newly opened State Botanical Garden of Georgia at the University of Georgia in Athens offers nature trails and rose and azalea gardens. The Fernbank Science Center in Atlanta features a botanical garden, a 65-acre (26-hectare) forest, natural-science exhibits and programs, and one of the largest planetariums in the nation.

National forestland covers about 60,000 acres (24,282 hectares) of Georgia land. More than 65,000 additional acres (26,305 hectares) are given over to national parks, monuments, and recreational areas, such as Cumberland Island National Seashore. In addition, Georgia has forty-three state parks and historic sites, most of which offer camping, hiking, fishing, water sports, and picnic facilities.

Historic Sites and Landmarks:

Andersonville National Historic Site, near Americus, is the site of the infamous Confederate prison where thirteen thousand Union prisoners died of exposure, starvation, and disease between 1864 and 1865. It includes Andersonville National Cemetery, the Confederate prison site, a museum, and state monuments.

Chickamauga and Chattanooga National Military Park, on U.S. 27 in the northwest corner of the state, is the nation's oldest and largest military park. Established by Congress in 1890, it commemorates the Civil War Battle of Chickamauga. The park includes hiking trails and a museum of military weaponry.

Fort Frederica National Monument, on St. Simons Island, was built by James Oglethorpe in 1736 and became the most expensive British fortification in the country. Here, Oglethorpe's greatly outnumbered colonists turned back Spanish invaders at the Battle of Bloody Marsh in 1742.

Fort Pulaski National Monument, near Savannah, honors Count Casimir Pulaski, the Polish hero of the American revolutionary war. Completed in 1847, the fort was used in the Civil War.

Jekyll Island Club Historic District, on Jekyll Island, is now a state-owned recreational area. From the late 1800s until the beginning of World War II, it was one of the world's most exclusive resorts, used by such elite families as the Vanderbilts, Goulds, Morgans, and Rockefellers. Today, many of the "cottage" retreats of the wealthy are restored and open to the public.

Kennesaw Mountain National Battlefield, near Marietta, commemorates one of the most decisive battles of the Civil War.

Little White House and Museum, at Warm Springs, was built by President Franklin Delano Roosevelt in 1932 so that he could be near the 82° F. (27.7° C) waters of Warm Springs for polio therapy. It was here that he died in April of 1945, while serving his fourth term in office.

Martin Luther King, Jr. National Historic Site, in Atlanta, honors the late civil-rights leader. It includes his birthplace; gravesite; the Ebenezer Baptist Church, where both he and his father were pastors; and the Freedom Hall Complex, home of the Martin Luther King, Jr. Center for Non-Violent Social Change.

Ocmulgee National Monument, near Macon, is the site of ancient Indian mounds. The archaeological museum there, one of the largest in the South, preserves ten thousand years of southeastern American Indian history.

Savannah Historic District is the nation's largest historic landmark district, with more than eleven hundred significant homes and buildings.

Other Interesting Places to Visit:

Amicalola Falls State Park, near Dawsonville, offers a view of Georgia's highest waterfall, as well as fishing, camping, and hiking.

Chehaw Wild Animal Park in Albany is a 100-acre (40.5-hectare) wildlife preserve designed by naturalist Jim Fowler. Protective trails and elevated walkways allow visitors a view of elk, bison, giraffes, elephants, coyotes, foxes, deer, and other animals in their natural habitats.

Etowah Indian Mounds, near Cartersville, consist of three large mounds and the remains of a fortified settlement and ceremonial capital thought to have been in use from about A.D. 1000 to 1500.

Georgia State Capitol in Atlanta houses the State Museum of Science and Industry, the Hall of Flags, and the Georgia Hall of Fame. The Capitol dome glows with gold leaf mined in Dahlonega, Georgia.

A gristmill at Stone Mountain Park near Atlanta

Kolomoki Indian Mounds and State Park, near Blakely, is a historic settlement dating from A.D. 800. It includes several burial, temple, and game mounds; a ceremonial plaza; and a museum depicting Indian cultures of the area.

Low House, in Savannah, is the former home of Juliette Gordon Low, who in 1912 founded the Girl Scouts of America. The white, stuccoed mansion has been restored as a showcase of Savannah life in the 1880s and is the national headquarters of the Girl Scouts organization.

New Echota, near Calhoun, was the last capital of the people of the Cherokee Nation before they were forcibly removed from Georgia to Oklahoma along the "Trail of Tears." The village has been partially restored.

Okefenokee Swamp, northeast of Fargo, is the site of the nation's largest wildlife refuge. Okefenokee Swamp Park features wildlife shows and boat trips.

Old State Capitol Museum, in Milledgeville, was used as the state capitol from 1804 to 1868. Nearby is the Old Governor's Mansion, built in 1838 and home to ten Georgia governors.

Plains is the hometown of former president Jimmy Carter. Points of interest are the Carter home, birthplace, campaign headquarters, and peanut warehouses.

Stone Mountain Memorial Park, near Atlanta, contains the world's largest single piece of sculptural art. Carved in the side of the granite mountain are the likenesses of Jefferson Davis, Robert E. Lee, and Thomas "Stonewall" Jackson.

The Rock House in Thomson, built about 1785, is Georgia's oldest documented dwelling. Built of stone, it dates from the Quaker migration to Wrightsborough, which began in 1768. It is restored as a house museum.

Westville, near Lumpkin, is a recreated 1850 Georgia village. Buildings of the period were moved there, restored, and furnished. Craftsmen demonstrate shoemaking, candlemaking, blacksmithing, and other nineteenth-century skills.

IMPORTANT DATES

8000 B.C.—Mound Builders begin building huge earthworks

A.D. 1000-1500—Cherokee people establish themselves in the plateaus; Creek inhabit the coastal plains

1540—Spanish expedition led by Hernando De Soto enters present-day Georgia

1562—French Huguenot explorer Jean Ribault explores the Georgia coast and claims it for the French

1565—Spanish captain Pedro Menéndez de Avilés drives out Ribault and the French Huguenots who have settled in Florida

1566—Menéndez builds a fort on Santa Catalina (Saint Catherines) Island

1680s—Creek Indians wipe out Spanish mission settlements

1721—Fort King George, the first English settlement in present-day Georgia, is built at the mouth of the Altamaha River

1732—King George II of England grants charter for the Colony of Georgia

1733—James Oglethorpe and his colonists arrive and negotiate a treaty with Chief Tomochichi for all the Creek Indian lands between the Savannah and Altamaha rivers; Savannah founded

1736—Augusta founded; fort established at Frederica

1742—Spanish influence in Georgia ends with the Battle of Bloody Marsh on St. Simons Island

1743—Oglethorpe leaves Georgia permanently

1750—Slave trade is allowed in Georgia

1754—Georgia becomes a royal province

1763—By the Treaty of Augusta, Indians cede land between the Savannah and Ogeechee rivers as far north as the Little River

1773—Creek and Cherokee Indians sign another treaty at Augusta, ceding to England 2.1 million acres (849,870 hectares) of present-day Georgia land

1775—Patriots calling themselves "Sons of Liberty" break into the Savannah powder magazine

1776—Three Georgians—Lyman Hall, George Walton, and Button Gwinnett—sign the Declaration of Independence

1777—First state constitution ratified; John Treutlen is elected first state governor

1778—British troops invade Georgia and capture Savannah

1781—The British are expelled from Augusta

1782—The British withdraw from Savannah, which once again becomes the seat of government

1785—The University of Georgia is chartered

1788—Georgia ratifies the United States Constitution and becomes the fourth state

1793—Eli Whitney invents the cotton gin while visiting a plantation near Savannah

1795—The Yazoo Fraud, a land grab involving members of the state legislature, is exposed

1801—First building of the University of Georgia is erected

1802—Georgia cedes lands west of the Chattahoochee River to the federal government

1814—General Andrew Jackson forces Creek Indians to sign treaty ceding land in southern Georgia

1819—The SS *Savannah*, the first steamship to cross the Atlantic, sails from Savannah to Liverpool, England

1825—The Creek are forced to cede to the federal government the last of their lands in Georgia

1828—Prospectors strike gold at Dahlonega, touching off the United States' first gold rush; the bilingual *Cherokee Phoenix* begins publication

1833—Construction of a railroad from Augusta to Union Point begins

1835—Congressman James H. Wayne of Georgia becomes an associate justice of the U.S. Supreme Court

1838—Federal troops force the Cherokee to leave Georgia; four thousand die along the "Trail of Tears" in the march westward

1842—First operation using ether as an anesthetic is performed by Dr. Crawford W. Long at Jefferson

1845—Georgia organizes its first supreme court

1847—Atlanta is incorporated as a city

1861—Georgia secedes from the Union; Alexander H. Stephens of Georgia elected vice-president of the Confederacy

1862—Union forces take Fort Pulaski and close the port of Savannah

1863—Confederate forces defeat Union forces at the Battle of Chickamauga

1864—General William T. Sherman invades Georgia, burns Atlanta, leads a march of destruction to the sea, and occupies Savannah

1865—Jefferson Davis, president of the Confederacy, is captured near Irwinville; Secession Ordinance is repealed; slavery is abolished

1867—Federal troops under Major General John Pope occupy Georgia; the Ku Klux Klan appears in the state; Atlanta University, Georgia's first black college, is granted a charter

1868—New state constitution establishes Atlanta as state capital

1870—Georgia is readmitted to the Union

1877—New state constitution adopted; Atlanta becomes the permanent state capital

1881—Atlanta hosts a World's Fair and International Cotton Exposition

1886—Atlanta druggist John Styth Pemberton develops the soft drink that will become Coca-Cola

1889—Present state capitol at Atlanta is opened

1907—Statewide prohibition of alcohol is adopted

1911—Joseph R. Lamar becomes an associate justice of the U.S. Supreme Court

1912—Juliette Gordon Low founds the Girl Scouts of America at Savannah

1914—Sixth District Federal Reserve Bank is established in Atlanta

1917—Georgia sends ninety-three thousand citizens to the military as the United States enters World War I

1921—Boll weevil epidemic seriously damages cotton crops

1922—Infantry training school is established at Fort Benning, near Columbus

1925—Georgia's first airport is established at Candler field in Atlanta

1928—Georgia's first commercial airways system is started

1934—Governor Talmadge calls in the National Guard against striking textile-mill workers

1943—Georgia becomes the first state to allow eighteen-year-olds to vote

1945—President Franklin D. Roosevelt dies at Warm Springs; new state constitution is adopted

1961—Atlanta begins token desegregation of public schools; blacks are admitted to the University of Georgia

1964—Dr. Martin Luther King, Jr. receives the Nobel Peace Prize

1969—Federal district court orders Georgia to create a racially balanced school system

1973—Maynard Jackson, Jr. is elected mayor of Atlanta, becoming the first black to be elected mayor of a large southern city

1976—New state constitution is adopted

1977—Jimmy Carter, former governor of Georgia, becomes the thirty-ninth president of the United States

1983—New state constitution goes into effect

1986—Georgia experiences its worst drought in nearly a century

1987—Cuban detainees at Atlanta Federal Penitentiary seize the compound and hold eighty-nine people hostage for eleven days after it is announced that the federal government intends to send them back to Cuba

IMPORTANT PEOPLE

Henry (Hank) Aaron (1934-   ), professional baseball player; joined the Milwaukee Braves in 1954 and moved to Georgia with the team when it became the Atlanta Braves in 1966; best known for breaking Babe Ruth's long-standing record of 714 home runs; received the NAACP's Springarn Medal in 1975; elected to the Baseball Hall of Fame in 1982

Conrad Potter Aiken (1889-1973), born in Savannah; poet, author; awarded 1930 Pulitzer Prize for *Selected Poems*; noted for the musiclike quality of his poetry, which most often deals with finding one's identity in a changing, unstable world

ABRAHAM BALDWIN

Abraham Baldwin (1754-1807), patriot; signed the United States Constitution on behalf of Georgia; helped found the state system of education; in 1785 helped found Franklin College (now the University of Georgia); United States representative (1790-99); United States senator (1799-1807)

Martha McChesney Berry (1866-1942), born near Rome; educator; used her own fortune and her skills as a fundraiser to establish schools for underprivileged children in the Georgia mountains; in Mount Berry founded a boarding school for boys (1902), a boarding school for girls (1909), and Berry College (1926)

MARTHA BERRY

Julian Bond (1940-   ), politician, civil-rights leader; helped found the Student Nonviolent Coordinating Committee (SNCC) in 1960, and served as its communications director (1961-66); Georgia state representative (1965-75); was one of the nominees for vice-president at the 1968 Democratic National Convention (although he was too young to hold the office); Georgia state senator (1975-   )

JULIAN BOND

James Nathaniel (Jim) Brown (1936-   ), born on St. Simons Island; professional football player; considered one of the greatest ball carriers of all time; led the National Football League in rushing in eight of the nine seasons he played; his career total of 12,312 yards rushing was the NFL record until 1984

Joseph Emerson Brown (1821-1894), politician; governor of Georgia (1857-65); after the Civil War joined the Republicans, promoted Reconstruction, and served as chief justice of Georgia (1868); United States senator (1880-91)

ERSKINE CALDWELL

Erskine Preston Caldwell (1903-1987), born in White Oak; writer; wrote *Tobacco Road, God's Little Acre,* and other stories of rural southern life

JIMMY CARTER

TY COBB

JOHN FRÉMONT

WALTER GEORGE

James Earl (Jimmy) Carter, Jr. (1924-   ), born in Plains; thirty-ninth president of the United States (1977-81); career naval officer who resigned in 1953 to manage his family's peanut business; governor of Georgia (1971-75); as governor streamlined state government and increased the number of blacks in government employ; as president, his domestic policies included pardoning Vietnam War draft evaders and adopting a national energy program to reduce the nation's dependence on oil imports; his foreign policies included supporting the worldwide struggle for human rights, bringing together the leaders of Egypt and Israel to negotiate a peace treaty in 1979, and securing treaties which will return control of the Panama Canal to Panama in 1999

Lucius DuBignon Clay (1897-1978), born in Marietta; army officer; commander in chief of United States armed forces in Europe and military governor of the United States military zone in Germany (1947-49); oversaw the Berlin Airlift, which brought food and supplies into Berlin in 1948

Howell Cobb (1815-1868), born in Cherry Hill; politician; United States representative (1843-51, 1855-57); Speaker of the House (1849-51); governor of Georgia (1851-53); United States secretary of the treasury (1857-60); president of the Confederate Congress (1861-62)

Tyrus Raymond (Ty) Cobb (1886-1961), born in Banks County; professional baseball player; nicknamed the Georgia Peach, he was with the Detroit Tigers as player (1905-26) and manager (1921-26); all-time leading major-league hitter with a lifetime batting average of .367 and twelve American League batting titles; his career total of 4,191 hits was the major-league record until 1985; elected to the Baseball Hall of Fame in 1936

Rebecca Latimer Felton (1835-1930), born near Decatur; author, political reformer; became the first woman United States senator when she served one day in 1922 as an interim appointee; noted for her articles in the *Atlanta Journal* and for her book *My Memoirs of Georgia Politics*

John Forsyth (1780-1841); lawyer, politician; United States representative (1813-18, 1823-27); United States senator (1818-19, 1829-34); United States minister to Spain (1819-23); governor of Georgia (1827-29); United States secretary of state (1834-41)

John Charles Frémont (1813-1890), born in Savannah; explorer, army officer, politician; became famous for exploring much of the area between the Rocky Mountains and the Pacific Ocean

Walter Franklin George (1878-1957), born near Preston; United States senator (1922-57); supported aid for foreign countries and greater international cooperation; was one of the first national leaders to call for a summit meeting of the Big Four (United States, Great Britain, France, and the Soviet Union) in 1955

John Brown Gordon (1832-1904), born in Upson County; soldier and politician; Confederate army general; United States senator (1873-80, 1891-97); governor of Georgia (1886-90)

Henry Woodfin Grady (1850-1889), born in Athens; journalist, orator; editor and part owner of the *Atlanta Constitution* (1879-89); worked for the rebuilding of the South after the Civil War; won national attention for his speech "The New South"

Nathanael Greene (1742-1786), revolutionary war general; commanded the Army of the South (1780-81) against the British so successfully that Georgia, North Carolina, and South Carolina honored him with gifts of large land grants; in 1785 retired to Mulberry Grove, the plantation given to him by Georgia

NATHANAEL GREENE

Button Gwinnett (1735-1777); merchant, plantation owner; signed the Declaration of Independence on behalf of Georgia; served in the Georgia Assembly (1769), the Continental Congress (1776, 1777), and as acting governor of Georgia (1777)

Joseph Habersham (1751-1815), born in Savannah; patriot, public official; member of the Georgia convention to ratify the United States Constitution (1788) and the Continental Congress (1785-86); United States postmaster general (1795-1801)

Lyman Hall (1724-1790), physician, patriot; signed the Declaration of Independence on behalf of Georgia; member of the Continental Congress (1775-78, 1780); governor of Georgia (1783)

JOEL CHANDLER HARRIS

William Joseph Hardee (1815-1873), born in Camden County; army officer; served with distinction in the Mexican War; resigned to become a Confederate army brigadier-general in the Civil War; his *Rifle and Light Infantry Tactics* was used as a textbook by both Union and Confederate officers

Joel Chandler Harris (1848-1908), born in Eatonton; journalist, author; astute observer of the folklore and speech patterns of southern blacks of his time; used his observations to create stories featuring such famous characters as Uncle Remus, Brer Rabbit, and Brer Fox; the Uncle Remus stories first appeared in the *Atlanta Constitution* and were later collected in a number of books

COURTNEY H. HODGES

Courtney Hicks Hodges (1887-1966), born in Perry; army officer; rose from rank of private in 1906 to four-star general in 1945; commanded the American First Army in World War II

John Hope (1868-1936), born in Augusta; educator; first black president of Morehouse College (1906-31); president of Atlanta University (1929-36); urged full social equality for blacks; encouraged young blacks to turn to a college education instead of vocational training; posthumously awarded the NAACP's Springarn Medal in 1936

Maynard Holbrook Jackson (1938-   ), politician; first black mayor of Atlanta (1974-81) and first black ever elected mayor of a major southern city

MAYNARD JACKSON

MARTIN LUTHER KING, JR.

JOSEPH LAMAR

JULIETTE GORDON LOW

CARSON MCCULLERS

Robert Tyre (Bobby) Jones, Jr. (1902-1971), born in Atlanta; professional golfer; only person to win the U.S. Open, the British Open, the U.S. Amateur, and the British Amateur tournaments all in one year, (1930); designed the Augusta National Golf Course

Martin Luther King, Jr. (1929-1968), born in Atlanta; clergyman, civil-rights leader; advocated demonstrating for social change through nonviolent means; in 1954 was ordained a Baptist minister; in 1957 founded the Southern Christian Leadership Conference, a civil-rights organization; as the main leader of the civil-rights movement in the 1950s and 1960s, led a series of nonviolent marches to end racial segregation and discrimination; a brilliant orator, he is especially remembered for his stirring speech "I Have A Dream," which he delivered to two hundred thousand people at the Lincoln Memorial after leading the massive March on Washington in 1963; under his leadership, the civil-rights movement won such victories as passage of the Civil Rights Act of 1964 and the Voting Rights Act of 1965; became the youngest person ever to win the Nobel Peace Prize (1964); assassinated in 1968 in Memphis; a federal holiday on the third Monday in January honors his birthday

Joseph Rucker Lamar (1857-1916), born in Elbert County; lawyer, jurist; Georgia state representative (1886-89); state supreme court justice (1904-06); associate justice of the U.S. Supreme Court (1911-16)

Lucy Laney (1854-1933), born in Macon, educator; founded a private school for black children in Augusta (1886) which became the Haines Normal and Industrial Institute

Sidney Lanier (1842-1881), born in Macon; poet; believed that a poem's sound was part of its excitement; best known for "The Marshes of Glynn," a poem describing a wild and swampy area near the Georgia coast

Crawford Williamson Long (1815-1878), born in Danielsville; surgeon; in 1842, while removing a tumor from the neck of a patient, became the first physician to use ether as an anesthetic

Juliette Gordon Low (1860-1927), born in Savannah; founder of the Girl Scouts of America; organized the first group of Girl Guides in the United States in Savannah in 1912 (renamed the Girl Scouts in 1913); first president of the Girl Scouts of America (1915-20)

Carson McCullers (1917-1967), born in Columbus; novelist; wrote about small-town southern life; best known for *The Heart Is a Lonely Hunter* and *The Member of the Wedding*

Ralph Emerson McGill (1898-1969), editor, publisher; editor (1942-60) and publisher (1960-69) of the *Atlanta Constitution*; awarded 1958 Pulitzer Prize for his editorial *The South and the Southerner*

Alexander McGillivray (1759?-1793), Chief of the Creek Federation; kept the southern Indian tribes loyal to England during the revolutionary war; allied with Spain to harass American settlements; although he signed a peace treaty with George Washington in 1790, he later broke it and began organizing a new war against the United States just before he died

Margaret Julia Mitchell (1900-1949), born in Atlanta; journalist, author; awarded the 1937 Pulitzer Prize in fiction for *Gone With the Wind*, a novel about life in the South during the Civil War; the book became one of the most popular novels of all time; in 1939 the book was turned into an award-winning movie

MARGARET MITCHELL

Elijah Muhammad (1897-1975), born Elijah Poole in Sandersville; leader of the Black Muslim movement; advocated the separation of blacks and whites; encouraged his followers to develop their own schools and businesses and to prove their character and morals by avoiding drugs, alcohol, tobacco, and pork

Mary Musgrove (1700?-1763?), born at Coweta Town; Creek Indian leader, trader; became General Oglethorpe's interpreter and representative among the Indians; influenced the Creek to remain loyal to the English in their struggle with Spain for what would become the southeastern United States

ELIJAH MUHAMMAD

Samuel (Sam) Nunn (1938-   ), born in Perry; politician; Georgia state representative (1968-72); United States senator (1972-   ); member of the Senate Steering Committee

Flannery O'Connor (1925-1964), born in Savannah; writer; her novels and short stories, set in the South, are peopled by haunted, violent, often physically or morally deformed characters; works include the novel *Wise Blood* and the short-story collections *A Good Man is Hard to Find* and *Everything That Rises Must Converge*

James Edward Oglethorpe (1696-1785), British philanthropist, soldier; founded the British colony of Georgia; arrived in 1733 and settled at Savannah, where he governed until 1743; organized the young colony; fought off Spanish attacks; in 1743 returned to England; in 1752 returned the Georgia charter to King George II

FLANNERY O'CONNOR

John Roosevelt (Jackie) Robinson (1919-1972), born near Cairo; professional baseball player; made history by becoming the first black player in the major leagues when he joined the Brooklyn Dodgers in 1947; led the Dodgers to six pennants and one world series; elected to the Baseball Hall of Fame in 1962

John Ross (1790-1866), Cherokee chief; first president of the National Council of Cherokees (1819-26); opposed the United States government's attempt to seize tribal lands and move the Cherokee west of the Mississippi; was forced in 1838 to lead his people along the "Trail of Tears"; chosen chief of the United Cherokee Nation in 1839; devoted the rest of his life to defending the rights and promoting the education of his exiled people

JACKIE ROBINSON

DEAN RUSK

TOMOCHICHI

ROBERT A. TOOMBS

HENRY MACNEAL TURNER

David (Dean) Rusk (1909-   ), born in Cherokee County; public official, professor; United States State Department official (from 1946); helped establish the Marshall Plan (aid to war-torn European countries following World War II) and NATO (North Atlantic Treaty Organization); United States secretary of state (1961-69); law professor at the University of Georgia (1970-   )

Sequoya (1760?-1843), silversmith, warrior, trader, scholar; in 1821 invented a written alphabet based on the sounds of his native Cherokee language; his system of writing enabled thousands of Cherokee to learn to read and write in their own language; devoted his life to helping his people; attempted to settle some of the bitter differences that arose among them after they were forced to move west

Charles Henry Smith (1826-1903), born in Lawrenceville; author, humorist; wrote "letters" in the persona of a country bumpkin named Bill Arp, whose illiterate dialect masked the sharp satire and wit of his comments; published weekly in the *Atlanta Constitution*, the letters were reprinted in national newspapers and collected into a series of books

Alexander Hamilton Stephens (1812-1883), born near Crawfordville; politician; United States representative (1843-59, 1873-82); vice-president of the Confederacy (1861-65); governor of Georgia (1882-83)

Eugene Talmadge (1884-1946), born in Forsyth; politician; governor of Georgia (1933-37, 1941-43); an energetic leader, he was known for his image as a "Georgia Cracker" who sported red suspenders and a "Cracker" speech style; called in the National Guard to put down textile-mill strikers; won a fourth term as governor in 1946, but died before taking office

Tomochichi (1664?-1739), Yamacraw chief; befriended Oglethorpe and aided the first British colonists by signing a formal treaty permitting the Savannah settlement; traveled with Oglethorpe to England, where he met King George II

Robert Augustus Toombs (1810-1885), born in Wilkes County; politician; United States representative (1843-53); United States senator (1853-61); staunch defender of the southern position on the slavery issue; led Georgia out of the Union; secretary of state of the Confederacy (1861); Confederate brigadier general (1861-62); after the Civil War, he refused to apply for pardon or to swear allegiance to the United States government, thus remaining an "unreconstructed rebel" for the rest of his life

Henry MacNeal Turner (1834-1915), born in Savannah; civil-rights leader; African Methodist Episcopal bishop; Union chaplain for black troops in the Civil War; served two terms in the Georgia assembly, where he fought for the rights of blacks and poor whites; promoted the black nationalist movement and the 1878 expedition of freed slaves to Liberia

Robert Edward (Ted) Turner III (1938-   ), broadcasting and sports executive, yachtsman; won the 1977 America's Cup in his yacht *Courageous*; president and chairman of the board of the Atlanta-based Turner Broadcasting System; president of the Atlanta Braves; chairman of the board of the Atlanta Hawks

Charles Walker (1858-1921), born in Hephzibah; Baptist minister, author; founded the "Colored YMCA" in New York City; in 1886 founded and became first pastor of the Baptist Institutional Church in Augusta, the largest black church in the United States at that time

George Walton (1741-1804), patriot, politician; signed the Declaration of Independence and the Articles of Confederation on behalf of Georgia; governor of Georgia (1779-80, 1789); chief justice of Georgia (1783-89); Georgia superior court justice (1790-95, 1799-1804); United States senator (1795-96)

Thomas Edward Watson (1856-1922), born in Columbus County near Thomson; editor, author, politician; represented populist sentiment in Georgia; United States representative (1891-93); introduced first bill passed to provide free rural mail delivery; Populist Party candidate for vice-president (1896) and president (1908); United States senator (1921-22)

James Moore Wayne (1790-1867), born in Savannah; soldier, politician, Georgia circuit court justice (1824-29); United States representative (1829-35); associate justice of the United States Supreme Court (1835-67)

Walter Francis White (1893-1955), born in Atlanta; author, civil-rights leader; secretary of the NAACP (1931-55); fought to end the lynching of blacks with such fiery books exposing racial prejudice as *A Man Called White*; awarded the NAACP's Springarn Medal in 1937

Eli Whitney (1765-1825), inventor; in 1793 developed the cotton gin (patented in 1794) while visiting the Savannah plantation of Mrs. Nathanael Greene; his invention, which mechanized the painstaking and time-consuming task of separating cotton seeds from fiber, revolutionized the cotton industry in the South

Frank Garvin Yerby (1916-   ), born in Augusta; author; wrote numerous historical novels; best-known work is *The Foxes of Harrow*

Andrew Jackson Young, Jr. (1932-   ), civil-rights leader, politician; executive director of the Southern Christian Leadership Conference (1964-70); chief aide of Dr. Martin Luther King, Jr.; United States representative (1972-77); first black to be appointed United States ambassador to the United Nations (1977-79); received the NAACP's Springarn Medal in 1978; mayor of Atlanta (1982-   )

TED TURNER

GEORGE WALTON

ELI WHITNEY

ANDREW YOUNG

GOVERNORS

John A. Treutlen	1777-1778	James Johnson	1865
John Houstoun	1778-1779	Charles J. Jenkins	1865-1868
John Wereat	1779-1780	Thomas H. Ruger	1868
George Walton	1779-1780	Rufus B. Bullock	1868-1871
Richard Howley	1780	Benjamin Conley	1871-1872
Stephen Heard	1780	James M. Smith	1872-1877
Myrick Davies	1780-1781	Alfred H. Colquitt	1877-1882
Nathan Brownson	1781-1782	Alexander H. Stephens	1882-1883
John Martin	1782-1783	James S. Boynton	1883
Lyman Hall	1783-1784	Henry D. McDaniel	1883-1886
John Houstoun	1784-1785	John B. Gordon	1886-1890
Samuel Elbert	1785-1786	William J. Northern	1890-1894
Edward Telfair	1786-1787	William Y. Atkinson	1894-1898
George Mathews	1787-1788	Allen D. Candler	1898-1902
George Handley	1788-1789	Joseph M. Terrell	1902-1907
George Walton	1789-1790	Hoke Smith	1907-1909
Edward Telfair	1790-1793	Joseph M. Brown	1909-1911
George Mathews	1793-1796	Hoke Smith	1911
Jared Irwin	1796-1798	John M. Slaton	1911-1912
James Jackson	1798-1801	Joseph M. Brown	1912-1913
David Emanuel	1801	John M. Slaton	1913-1915
Josiah Tattnall, Jr.	1801-1802	Nathaniel E. Harris	1915-1917
John Milledge	1802-1806	Hugh M. Dorsey	1917-1921
Jared Irwin	1806-1809	Thomas W. Hardwick	1921-1923
David B. Mitchell	1809-1813	Clifford Walker	1923-1927
Peter Early	1813-1815	Lamartine G. Hardman	1927-1931
David B. Mitchell	1815-1817	Richard B. Russell, Jr.	1931-1933
William Rabun	1817-1819	Eugene Talmadge	1933-1937
Matthew Talbot	1819	Eurith D. Rivers	1937-1941
John Clark	1819-1823	Ellis G. Arnal	1943-1947
George M. Troup	1823-1827	Melvin E. Thompson	1947-1948
John Forsyth	1827-1829	Herman E. Talmadge	1948-1955
George R. Gilmer	1829-1831	Marvin Griffin	1955-1959
Wilson Lumpkin	1831-1835	Ernest Vandiver	1959-1963
William Schley	1835-1837	Carl E. Sanders	1963-1967
George R. Gilmer	1837-1839	Lester G. Maddox	1967-1971
Charles J. McDonald	1839-1843	James E. Carter, Jr.	1971-1975
George W. Crawford	1843-1847	George D. Busbee	1975-1983
George W. Towns	1847-1851	Joe Frank Harris	1983-
Howell Cobb	1851-1853		
Herschel V. Johnson	1853-1857		
Joseph E. Brown	1857-1865		

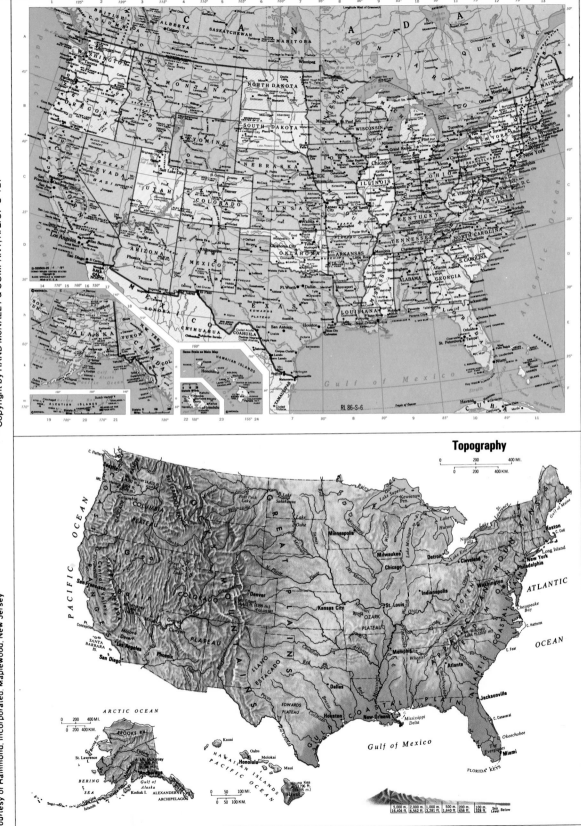

RL 86-S-6

Topography

MAP KEY

Acworth	B2	Cornelia	B3
Adel	E3	Covington	C3
Ailey	D4	Crawford	C3
Alapaha River (river)	E,F3	Crawfordville	C4
Albany	E2	Cumberland Island (island)	F5
Alcovy River (river)	C3	Cumming	B2
Allatoona Lake (Lake)	B2	Cusseta	D2
Alma	E4	Cuthbert	E2
Alpharetta	B2	Dacula	C3
Altamaha River (river)	E4,5	Dahlonega	B3
Americus	D2	Dallas	C2
Arnoldsville	C3	Dalton	B2
Ashburn	E3	Danville	D3
Athens	C3	Darien	E5
Atlanta	C2;h8	Dawson	E2
Atlantic Ocean	E,F5,6	Dearing	C4
Augusta	C4,5	Decatur	C2;h8
Austell	h7	Demorest	B3
Avondale Estates	h8	Dexter	D4
Axson	E4	Donalsonville	E2
Bainbridge	F2	Doraville	h8
Baldwin	B3	Douglas	E4
Banks Lake (lake)	E,F3	Douglasville	C2
Barnesville	C2	Dublin	D4
Baxley	E4	Duluth	B2;g,h8
Bibb City	D2	Dunwoody	h8
Big Satilla Creek (creek)	E4,5	East Ellijay	B2
Blackbeard Island (island)	E5	East Newnan	C2
Blackshear	E4	East Point	C2;h7
Blairsville	B3	Eastman	D3
Blakely	E2	Eatonton	C3
Bloomingdaie	D5	Edison	E2
Blue Ridge	B2	Elberta	D3
Blue Ridge Lake (lake)	B2	Elberton	B4
Bogart	C3	Ellaville	D2
Boston	F3	Ellijay	B2
Bowden	C1	Emerson	B2
Bowman	B3	Enigma	E3
Brasstown Bald Mountain (mountain)	B3	Etowah River (river)	B2
Bremen	C1	Experiment	C2
Broad River (river)	B,C3,4	Fair Oaks	h7
Bronwood	E2	Fairburn	C2;h7
Brooklet	D5	Fairmount	B2
Broxton	E4	Fayetteville	C2
Brunswick	E5	Fitzgerald	E3
Buchanan	C1	Flint River (river)	C,D,E,F2,3
Buena Vista	D2	Flowery Branch	B3
Buford	B2	Folkston	F4
Bull Sluice Lake (lake)	g,h8	Forest Park	h8
Butler	D2	Forsyth	C3
Byromville	D3	Fort Benning	D2
Byron	D3	Fort Gaines	E1
Cairo	F2	Fort Gordon	C4
Calhoun	B2	Fort Oglethorpe	B1
Camilla	E2	Fort Stewart	D5
Canon	B3	Fort Valley	D3
Canoochee River (river)	D4,5	Franklin	C1
Canton	B2	Fulton River (river)	B,C1,2
Carters Lake (lake)	B2	Gainesville	B3
Cartersville	B2	Garden City	D5
Cave Spring	B1	Georgetown	E1
Cedartown	B1	Gibson	C4
Center	B3	Glennville	E5
Centralhatchee	C1	Glenwood	D4
Chamblee	h8	Gordon	D3
Charing	D2	Grantville	C2
Charlotteville	D4	Gray	C3
Chatsworth	B2	Greensboro	C3
Chattahoochee River (river)	B,C2,3;D,E,F1,2;h7,8	Greenville	C2
Chatuge Lake (lake)	A,B3	Griffin	C2
Chickamauga	B1	Groveland	D5
Clark Hill Lake (reservoir)	C4	Grovetown	C4
Clarkston	h8	Guyton	D5
Clarksville	B3	Hagan	D5
Claxton	D5	Hahira	F3
Clayton	B3	Hamilton	D2
Cleveland	B3	Hampton	C2
Cobbtown	D4	Hapeville	C2;h8
Cochran	D3	Hardwick	C3
Colbert	B3	Harlem	C4
College Park	C2;h8	Hartwell	B4
Collins	D4	Hawkinsville	D3
Colquitt	E2	Hazlehurst	E4
Columbus	D2	Helena	D4
Comer	B3	Hephzibah	C4
Commerce	B3	Hilltonia	C4
Conyers	C2;h8	Hinesville	E5
Coosa River (river)	B1	Hiram	C2
Coosawattee River (river)	B1,2	Hoboken	E4
Cordele	E3	Hogansville	C2
		Holly Springs	B2

Homeland		Quitman	F3
Homer		Ray City	E3
Homerville		Reidsville	D4
Ideal		Reynolds	D2
Irwinton		Rhine	E3
Isabella		Richland	D2
Jackson		Richmond Hill	E5
Jackson Lake (lake)		Rincon	D5
Jasper		Ringgold	B1
Jefferson		Roberta	D2
Jeffersonville		Rochelle	E3
Jekyll Island (island)	--	Rockmart	B1
Jesup	E5	Rome	B1
Jonesboro	C2	Rossville	B1
Kennesaw	B2;g7	Roswell	B2;g8
Kingsland	F5	Royston	B3
Kingston	B2	Rutledge	C3
La Fayette	B1	Saint Catherines Island (island)	E5
La Grange	C1	Saint Marys	F5
Lake Blackshear (lake)	E3	Saint Simons Island (island)	E5
Lake Burton (lake)	B3	Sandersville	D4
Lake Seminole (lake)	F2	Sandy Springs	h8
Lake Sidney Lanier (lake)	B2,3	Sapelo Island (island)	E5
Lake Sinclair (lake)	C3	Sardis	D5
Lakeland	E3	Satilla River (river)	E,F4,5
Lavonia	B3	Savannah	D5
Lawrenceville	C3;h9	Savannah River (river)	B3,B,C4,C,D5
Leary	E2	Scottdale	h8
Leesburg	E2	Screven	E4
Lenox	E3	Senoia	C2
Lilburn	h8	Shannon	B1
Lincoln Park	D2	Shellman	E2
Lincolnton	C4	Siloam	C3
Lindale	B1	Smithville	E2
Lithia Springs	h7	Smyrna	C2;h7
Lithonia	C2;h8	Social Circle	C3
Little River (river)	C3,4	Soperton	D4
Little River (river)	E,F3	South River (river)	h8
Little Tallapoosa River (river)	C1,2	Sparks	E3
Locust Grove	C2	Sparta	C4
Loganville	C3	Springfield	D5
Louisville	C,D4	Statesboro	D5
Ludowici	E5	Statham	C3
Lula	B3	Stillmore	D4
Lumber City	E4	Stockbridge	C2
Lumpkin	D2	Stockton	F3
Luthersville	C2	Stone Mountain (mountain)	C2;h8
Lyons	D4	Sugar Hill	B2
Mableton	h7	Summerville	B1
Macon	D3	Suwanee	B2
Madison	C3	Suwannee River (river)	F4
Manchester	D2	Swainsboro	D4
Marietta	C2;h7	Sycamore	E3
Marshallville	D3	Sylvania	D5
Martinez	C4	Sylvester	E3
Maysville	B3	Talbotton	D2
McCaysville	B2	Tallapoosa	C1
McDonough	C2	Temple	C1
McRae	D4	Tennille	D4
Meigs	E2	Thomaston	D2
Menlo	B1	Thomasville	F3
Metter	D4	Thomson	C4
Midville	D4	Thunderboldt	D5
Milan	D3	Tifton	E3
Milledgeville	C3	Tignall	C4
Millen	D5	Toccoa	B3
Monroe	C3	Toccoa River (river)	B2
Montezuma	D2	Toomsboro	D3
Monticello	C3	Trenton	B1
Morrow	C2;h8	Trion	B1
Moultrie	E3	Tucker	h8
Mount Airy	B3	Tunnel Hill	B1
Mount Vernon	D4	Twin City	D4
Mountain City	B3	Ty Ty	E3
Mount Berry	B1	Unadilla	D3
North Atlanta	h8	Union City	C2;h7
Nahunta	E5	Union Point	C3
Nashville	E3	Uvalda	D4
Nelson	B2	Valdosta	F3
Newnan	C2	Vidalia	D4
Newton	E2	Vienna	D3
Nicholls	E4	Villa Rica	C1
Norcross	C2;h8	Waco	C1
Norman Park	E3	Wadley	D4
Nottely Lake (reservoir)	B2,3	Waleska	B2
Oakwood	B3	Walthourville	E5
Ochlockonee	F2	Warm Springs	D2
Ochlockonee River (river)	F2,3	Warner Robins	D3
Ocilla	E3	Warrenton	C4
Ocmulgee River (river)	C,D,E3,4	Warwick	E3
Oconee River (river)	C,D3,4	Washington	C4
Ogeechee River (river)	C,D,E4,5	Watkinsville	C3
Oglethorpe	D2	Waverly Hall	D2
Ohoopee River (river)	D,E4	Waycross	E4
Okefenokee Swamp (swamp)	F4	Waynesboro	C4
Omega	E3	Weiss Reservoir (reservoir)	B1
Ossabaw Island (island)	E5	West Point	D1
Oxford	C3	West Point Reservoir (reservoir)	C,D1,2
Palmetto	C2	Whigham	F2
Patterson	E4	White	B2
Pavo	F3	Whitesburg	C2
Pearson	E4	Willacoochee	E3
Pelham	E2	Winder	C3
Pembrooke	D5	Winterville	C3
Perry	D3	Withlacoochee River (river)	E,F3
Pine Lake	h8	Woodbine	F5
Pine Mountain	D2	Woodbury	D2
Pineview	D3	Woodland	D2
Plains	D2	Woodstock	B2
Pooler	D5	Woodville	C3
Port Wentworth	D5	Wrens	C4
Portal	D5	Wrightsville	D4
Porterdale	C3	Yellow River (river)	g,h8
Poulan	E3	Young Harris	B3
Powder Springs	h7	Zebulon	C2

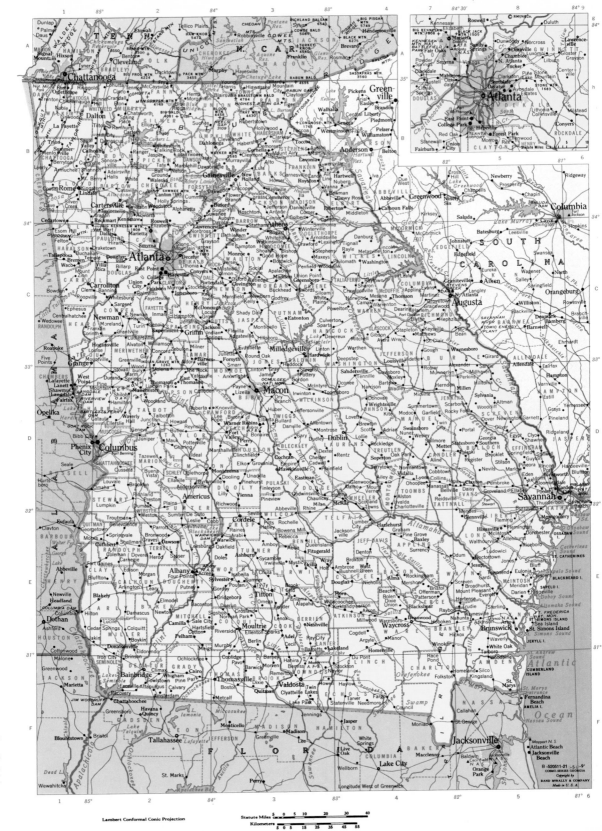

Lambert Conformal Conic Projection

Statute Miles

Kilometers

COTTON
MILK
GRAPES
TOBACCO
SHRIMP
VEGETABLES
FRUIT
SOYBEANS
OATS
FOREST PRODUC
WHEAT
HOGS
CORN
BEEF
POULTRY
MINING
BERRIES
SORGHUM GRAIN

MANUFACTURING
PEANUTS
PECANS
SWEET POTATOES

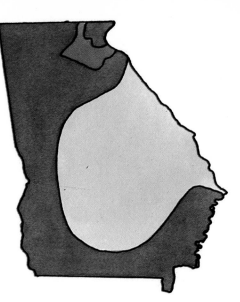

AVERAGE YEARLY PRECIPITATION		
Centimeters		Inches
163 to 183		64 to 72
142 to 163		56 to 64
122 to 142		48 to 56
102 to 122		40 to 48

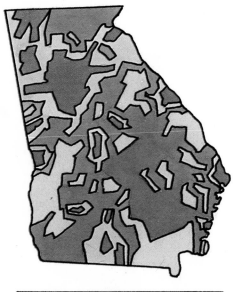

POPULATION DENSITY		
Number of persons per square kilometer		Number of persons per square mile
more than 40		more than 100
20 to 40		50 to 100
10 to 20		25 to 50
Less than 10		Less than 25

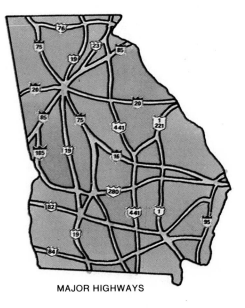

MAJOR HIGHWAYS

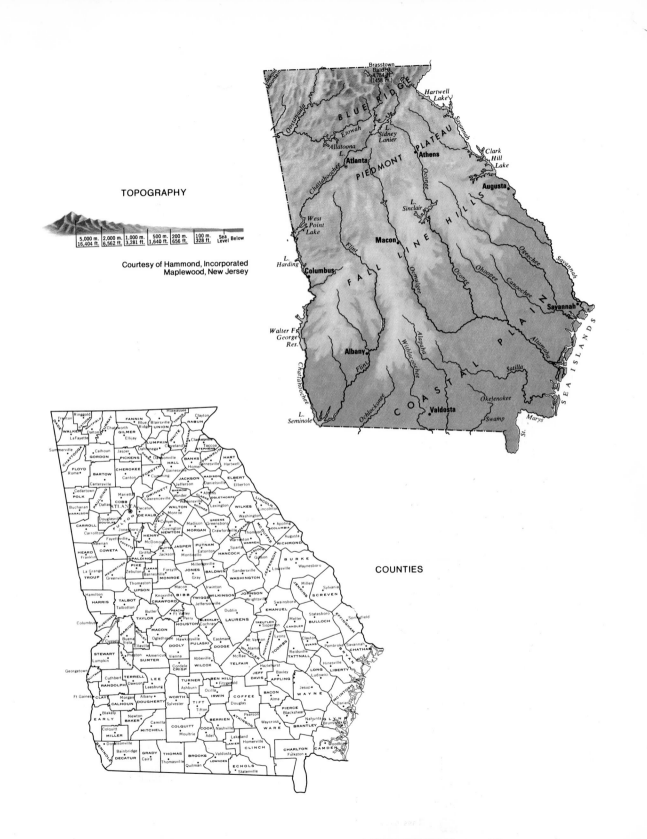

TOPOGRAPHY

5,000 m.	2,000 m.	1,000 m.	500 m.	200 m.	100 m.	Sea
16,404 ft.	6,562 ft.	3,281 ft.	1,640 ft.	656 ft.	328 ft.	Level	Below

Courtesy of Hammond, Incorporated
Maplewood, New Jersey

COUNTIES

Shrimp boats in southeast Georgia

INDEX

Page numbers that appear in boldface type indicate illustrations.

A general store near Athens

Picture Identifications
Front cover: Atlanta's Peachtree Center
Back cover: Okefenokee Swamp
Pages 2-3: Black Rock Mountain State Park in northeast Georgia
Page 6: Georgia peaches
Pages 8-9: Cumberland Island National Seashore
Page 18: Montage of Georgia residents
Page 24: Savannah as it appeared in 1734
Page 36: Count Casimir Pulaski receives a fatal wound during the 1779 siege of Savannah
Pages 46-47: The Battle of Lookout Mountain
Page 58: Interior of the main building of the 1881 International Cotton Exposition in Atlanta
Pages 72-73: Skyline of Atlanta showing the gold-domed State Capitol
Page 81: Atlanta's High Museum of Art
Pages 92-93: Helen, an Alpine-style village in the northern mountain region
Page 108: Montage showing the state flag, the state tree (live oak), the state flower (cherokee rose), the state bird (brown thrasher), and the state insect (honeybee)

Picture Acknowledgments

H. Armstrong Roberts, Inc.: Front cover; © W. Metzen: Back cover
Jerry Hennen: Pages 2-3, 15 (opossum, deer), 110
©**Journalism Services:** © Mike Kidulich: Pages 4, 107 (right); © Dave Brown: Page 18 (bottom left); © Paul Burd: Pages 51 (left), 141; © Max & Bea Hunn: Pages 89 (left), 95 (right), 96 (right), 103
Root Resources: © Pat Canova: Pages 5, 54 (top right), 83, 90; © David Dobbs: Pages 6, 78, 81, 117; © Bill Thomas: Pages 8-9; © Edna Douthat: Pages 13 (right), 105 (both photos); © Mary A. Root: Pages 15 (azalea), 108 (cherokee rose); © Marshall Brown: Page 18 (top right); © Bill Barksdale: Page 23 (left); © J.H. Robinson: Pages 53 (right), 113 (right), 115 (left); © Don & Pat Valenti: Page 108 (bee)
Roloc Color Slides: Pages 11, 26 (left), 30 (right), 41, 49, 51 (right), 53 (left), 77 (left), 89 (right), 95 (left), 96 (left), 118
Nawrocki Stock Photo: © R. Perron: Page 106 (left); © Fred Whitehead: Pages 12, 13 (left), 18 (bottom right), 54 (bottom right), 92-93, 107 (left), 108 (tree), 120, 138
© **Lynn M. Stone:** Pages 15 (turkey, mountain laurel, alligator, snake, gayfeather), 16, 113 (left)
Cameramann International Ltd.: Pages 18 (top left), 23 (right), 67, 75 (right), 77 (right), 88, 97 (right), 115 (right)
Marilyn Gartman Agency: © Michael Philip Manheim: Page 18 (middle)
Historical Pictures Service, Inc., Chicago: Pages 24, 28, 30 (left), 31, 32, 34, 36, 39 (both photos), 44 (both photos), 45, 46-47, 54 (top left, bottom left), 56, 58, 60, 63, 65, 85, 127 (Greene, Harris), 128 (King, Lamar), 130 (all photos), 131 (Walton)
Photri: Pages 26 (right), 42, 68, 71, 126 (Carter)
© **Jo Davidson:** Page 49
Wide World Photos: Pages 66, 125 (all photos), 126 (Cobb, Frémont, George), 127 (Hodges, Jackson), 128 (Low, McCullers), 129 (all photos), 131 (Turner, Whitney, Young)
SuperStock International: Pages 72-73, 97 (left), 98, 99, 100, 102, 106 (right)
© **Chandler Forman:** Page 75 (left)
Animals, Animals: © Ron Willocks: Page 108 (brown thrasher)
Len W. Meents: Maps on pages 96, 99, 102, 103, 105, 136
Courtesy Flag Research Center, Winchester, Massachusetts 01890: Flag on page 108

About the Author

Zachary Kent grew up in Little Falls, New Jersey. He is a graduate of St. Lawrence University and holds a teaching certificate in English. After college, he worked for two years at a New York City literary agency before launching his writing career. He is the author of eighteen books of American history and biography for young people.

As a Civil War buff, Mr. Kent once spent a long and happy vacation crisscrossing Georgia and visiting many of its historic sites. In preparation for this book, he again traveled to Georgia. The state's beautiful scenery, kind people, and exciting heritage have left him deeply impressed.